Perfectly Imperfect Puppy

Graeme Hall

Perfectly Imperfect Puppy

Graeme Hall

The ultimate life-changing programme for training a well-behaved, happy dog

3

Ebury Spotlight, an imprint of Ebury Publishing
20 Vauxhall Bridge Road
London SW1V 2SA

Ebury Spotlight is part of the Penguin Random House group of companies whose addresses can be found at global.penguinrandomhouse.com

Copyright © Graeme Hall 2022

Design by Emily Voller
Illustrations © Hannah Fleetwood
Photography © Cristian Barnett

Graeme Hall has asserted his right to be identified as the author of this Work in accordance with the Copyright, Designs and Patents Act 1988

The information in this book has been compiled as general guidance on dog training. It is not a substitute and not to be relied on for professional advice. So far as the author is aware the information given is correct and up to date as of 22/11/2021. The author and publishers disclaim, as far as the law allows, any liability arising directly or indirectly from the use, or misuse, of the information contained in this book.

First published by Ebury Spotlight in 2022

www.penguin.co.uk

A CIP catalogue record for this book is available from the British Library

ISBN 9781529149210

Printed and bound in Great Britain by Clays Ltd, Elcograf S.p.A.
The authorised representative in the EEA is Penguin Random House Ireland, Morrison Chambers, 32 Nassau Street, Dublin D02 YH68

Penguin Random House is committed to a sustainable future for our business, our readers and our planet. This book is made from Forest Stewardship Council® certified paper.

To Mollie Hall, aka Mum.
In gratitude for your patience
and perseverance when I was a
mischievous puppy.

Contents

CHAPTER 2. GETTING READY FOR YOUR PUPPY

CHAPTER 3. BRINGING YOUR PUPPY HOME

CHAPTER 4. SOCIALISING YOUR PUPPY

CHAPTER 5. PUPPY TRAINING!

CHAPTER 6. YOUR PUPPY'S HEALTH AND GROOMING

CHAPTER 7. DOG DAYS
(OR WHEN THEY START TO GROW UP)

Introduction

Hi there, pup-pickers! Graeme Hall here. You probably know me as The Dogfather, that tall bloke off the telly who wears a cravat and helps people get their dogs to stop doing naughty things. That's me! But working with slightly mischievous adult dogs is only a small part of what I do. A big part of my 15-year dog training career has always been about helping dog owners to choose, look after and train their new puppies.

I love puppies! Who doesn't? It's a cold-hearted person who's immune to the charms of a loving, snuggly, bundle-of-chaos puppy. And if I ever retire from dog training, I'm sure it will be the lovely biscuity smell of puppies – and the laughter that always comes with them – that I miss most.

I also love working with puppies because there is so much potential to make a lasting difference to a dog's life and to their owner's. There's an old saying: 'You only get one chance to make a first impression,' and I always think puppy training is a bit like that. Don't get me wrong, I firmly believe that you can train any dog at any age, and I'm very proud of the fact I never expelled a dog from one of my classes. But if you can get it right, or right-ish, when they are a puppy, you are paving the way for a lifetime of reliably good, and safe, behaviour.

Having said that, the word 'training' increasingly feels like a bit of a misnomer to me. Because for me, having a dog is about building a partnership, and about communication, not about creating a robot. Having managed staff in huge factories and spent many years as a Special Constable, I've learned that good leadership isn't about forcing your workforce, or your braying crowd, to do something, it's about creating a desire within them to want to do the right thing.

The best boss you ever had didn't shout at you or push you or shove you, although you probably wouldn't have wanted to get on the wrong side of them either! Subtle, calm and assertive communication – especially body language and tone of voice – will always beat bullying and demands.

And for me the same principles apply in dog training. So when we talk about 'training', what we're really talking about is establishing an understanding between you and your animal, talking in a language that you both speak fluently, even though you are from two entirely different species. Rather than a dog who 'does what they're told', I'm always aiming for a dog who understands, anticipates and responds to you.

Back when I started working with dogs, this kind of thinking was frowned upon in training and behaviour circles, where the anthropomorphisation of our dogs was considered sentimental and somehow wrong. The style back then was more authoritarian – you were meant to be the pack leader, which in reality meant bullying your dog into submission or, in the worst cases, brutalising them.

Thankfully, dog training has come a long way since then and I have worked with literally thousands of puppies, from the greatest of Great Danes to the tiniest of teacup toy breeds. But, perhaps, the two puppies who have taught me most about the joys and pains of raising young dogs are my own two Rottweilers, Axel and Gordon, who I had the privilege of owning from the mid-2000s.

Why did I choose Rottweilers? People often ask me this. They do say that people go for dogs who reflect their own personalities. I guess being quite tall, I've always felt an affinity with big dogs. And having spent time with my then-partner's Rottweiler, Hooch, I came to realise that Rotties have a big presence but are, generally speaking, cuddly teddy bears lurking under a lot of bravado. Make of that what you will!

Sadly, Hooch passed away in October 2005; we were both grief-stricken and thought it would be some time before either of us was ready to take on another dog. 'We' decided we'd spend the money on a nice white sofa instead and enjoy the clean house and the relative peace and quiet of a dog-free home for a while.

Then, just a few weeks later, our house was burgled and quite a few items of sentimental value were taken.

As a Special Constable in the police force, I knew from experience what a great deterrent a dog in the house can be against burglaries and unwelcome visitors of any kind.

We decided that maybe we'd look around for a Rottweiler breeder after all. That was in October 2005. We found a Kennel Club-listed breeder, based on the south coast, and went to see the puppies two or three times before we finally took young Axel home in February 2006. In fact, the first time I met him he was about three weeks old, and I could hold him in the palm of my hand. By the time he was fully grown, he was a 50kg dog and that was, unsurprisingly, no longer possible.

I often talk about that breeder, and the process of choosing Axel, as a great example of how the puppy-buying process should go. The breeder was extremely caring and proud of her dogs, and each time we visited it felt as though we were being interviewed for a very important job. This is how it should be. She really was concerned about where the puppy would be going and how suitable we were going to be as owners. In the end, I felt that she was so attuned to the animals and concerned about their future that I asked her to recommend which puppy we should take home from the litter. I always think that, if you can, it's best to build a good relationship with the breeder you are buying from so that they can guide you on which puppy is best suited to you (more on choosing the perfect breeder in Chapter 1).

Axel's show name was Quebex Atticus, but we called him Axel because we got stuck behind a huge hauling lorry on the drive home and my partner suggested, jokingly, that we call him 'back axle'. After laughing at first, it occurred to me that Axel actually is a German boy's name and by the time we got moving again, he had been christened Axel (there's also more on choosing names in Chapter 2).

So, I had done everything the correct way: a reputable breeder, a long cooling-off period to ensure we weren't making an impulse purchase, and plenty of visits to get to know the puppy before we took him home.

In August of the same year, I did it all the wrong way. I got a call from a bloke I knew in Yorkshire who ran a kennel. He had a problem that he was hoping I could fix: two of the Rottweilers he kept on-site had mated – a pair of teenagers in love – and he now had a litter of puppies on his hands. He knew I worked with the police force and was keen to find out if the dogs might be of interest to the local Dog Unit. He was concerned because the parents were both protection dogs, with the kind of temperaments you don't typically associate with family-friendly pets. He, very responsibly, didn't want the dogs to go to an inexperienced family or anyone who couldn't handle them properly.

A few weeks later, I found myself driving up to Yorkshire to pick up a puppy I'd never met, who at seven weeks old was not at the recommended age to be taken home, and was also from an unregistered breeder. Still, they were free to a good home, and free is the Yorkshireman's favourite price of all!

I give that story as an example of how not to do it, but also to demonstrate that even the most seasoned of dog owners can be seduced by the lure of a cute puppy (especially if it's free, although it's hard to imagine such a thing as a free puppy these days). It's also a good example of how what you look for in a puppy can change according to your own situation at home. Had I not already had Axel, I might have gone home with a different pup. But, again, I asked the breeder to choose a puppy from the litter based on the information I gave him about Axel. With Axel already being top dog at home, I knew I needed a puppy who was prepared to be, at the very least, slightly subordinate. When I picked him up, the guy suggested I take the little one with the flash of white on his chest, who he, rather unimaginatively I felt, had been calling Flash. I decided he wouldn't be called Flash, but Gordon (you need to be of a certain age to get that reference). The breeder needn't have been worried about Gordon's temperament, he turned out to be the goofiest, softest big baby I've ever known.

Having two male Rottweilers at home and knowing the size that they would both eventually become, made me resolve to do everything I could to train them properly early on. So, I joined a dog training club with Gordon and Axel, which made me quite quickly realise that this was something I wanted to do full-time. I took a canine behaviour management course, got myself listed with the Kennel Club and, a year or so later, I was running my own puppy training classes in the hall at Earls Barton Youth Club. And the rest, as they say, is history.

Having Rottweilers was also interesting from a psychology point of view. People tend to think of these dogs as big, aggressive and dangerous. They can be all these things, in the wrong hands. But as most Rottie owners will tell you, they are mostly just big galoots who want to slobber over and cuddle you all day long. This raises an interesting and age-old question: is behaviour something puppies are born already programmed with or is it something they learn? The old nature versus nurture debate has been going since Sigmund Freud was in short trousers. A few years ago, I put a poll up on my Facebook page asking dog owners whether they thought their dogs behaved as they did because of the way they had been trained or because of their innate nature? Debate raged for days but very few people came up with what I consider to be the right answer, which is, of course, a bit of both.

Successfully raising a puppy will depend on the raw materials you are working with – the breed and its built-in characteristics – but also the way in which you lead them to good behaviour. It won't always be a straight fifty-fifty, but it will always be a mixture of both. There's plenty of advice over the next few chapters about how to work with your dog's existing good nature and to nurture more good nature on top.

Of course, there is also plenty of advice on training a puppy available on the internet, and at the bar of every pub in the land. But, in my experience, there is so much advice – much of it conflicting – that it can become all too confusing. Do dogs need neutering? Should you brush their teeth? Is a harness better than a collar? Everyone has an opinion. And most puppy training books seem to make a lot of false promises about what can realistically be achieved. I've been training dogs for years and have met a lot of puppies in my time; I am yet to come across one who behaved consistently, perfectly, at all times. Like us humans, especially the young ones, puppies are all about exploration, experimentation, boundless energy and exuberance – none of these things tends to be easy to consistently manage, particularly if and when you already have a busy life.

With this book, I really wanted to be more realistic about the expectations we all have when training a puppy. There is going to be a lot of mess, you're going to lose some shoes, you're probably going to cry at some point, you're definitely going to fail at something, somewhere along the line. Let's get real about the demanding but incredibly rewarding process of bringing a small creature like this into your life. And, also, let's demystify the puppy experience with clear, simple advice, based on science and experience, not a set of rigid instructions and magical claims.

I find it fascinating to think that all dogs were once puppies and, just like us, they've all got a story, a set of circumstances, that brings them into the world and eventually through your front door, into your heart. As a boy growing up in Yorkshire, I was always taught that if a job's worth doing, it's worth doing well. Although sound advice on many levels, it tends to lean towards a kind of perfectionism that is pretty much impossible to achieve, both in life and in puppy training. As a grown-up who has travelled the length and breadth of the country working with dogs, I've learned that perfection is not only pretty much impossible, but it's an expectation that sets you up for disappointment and regret in the long run. (That, and that there's no place like Yorkshire.)

A far better way, then, is to always do the best that you can and expect this puppy training business to be tiring and difficult, as well as lovely and funny. And accept that while the perfect puppy probably doesn't exist, the perfectly *imperfect* puppy, who is perfect just for you, and who thinks you're pretty perfect too, is the best kind of puppy there is.

Chapter 1

Choosing Your Puppy

Puppies, puppies, everywhere.
But which one is perfect for you?

Do I Need a Dog?

Before you begin to think about the kind of puppy that might be right for you, it's worth taking a moment to consider why you might want one at all. Just think about it for a sec: *Why exactly do I want a puppy?*

Of course, there is no right or wrong answer; I can't tell you why you *should* want one. But what I can tell you are a couple of the reasons I regularly hear from potential puppy parents that tend to set alarm bells ringing for me.

Not a non-stop party

The first is the entertainment factor. People imagine a puppy will bring some laughs and a distracting novelty into their lives – maybe they've watched everything on Netflix or they're beginning to find their partner a little bit dull, and fancy seeing a new face around the place. I get it, I really do, but I've yet to meet a puppy who is the solution to any of those problems. Dogs, especially baby ones, are undeniably entertaining and loads of fun, we all love their mischievous nature and general cuteness. But no matter how much of a loveable rogue your puppy is, the entertainment factor is only one part of the package. And arguably it's a very small part, one that gets routinely overshadowed by the other, more demanding, far less rewarding aspects of raising a young animal in your home (we'll come on to those shortly).

Not an alternative to the gym

The other thing I hear a lot is people who say they want a puppy (and the thing the puppy eventually grows into, aka a dog) because they want the exercise. This is another noble and entirely understandable reason for owning a puppy, but again, in my opinion it's not something that should form the bedrock of the relationship you are about to em-bark (excuse the pun) on. I always say to people: if you're putting on weight then your dog's not getting enough exercise. And it's true, if you're signing up for this you need to be prepared to put in the hours, and the miles, that your dog needs and deserves. But a puppy is so much more than a reason to get out of the house. They spend a lot of time with you *in* the house, for starters. And they do not come exercise-ready, with road safety skills and a copy of the Highway Code. Before you can rely on them for your personal training needs, they'll need a lot of personal training themselves. So by all means, enjoy getting out and about with your pup, but be absolutely clear that owning a dog is about so much more than taking them for walks and improving your fitness.

Not a fashion accessory

The way a dog looks always seems to crop up as well. I once met a family who had found themselves struggling to cope with two Akitas (Japanese guard dogs bred to hunt bears; all soft and cuddly on the outside, erstwhile assassins on the inside). When I asked them why they'd decided to go for this particular breed, they said they'd originally wanted rabbits because they wanted something fluffy to cuddle. But after seeing Akitas in a film, while out at the cinema, decided that they looked fluffier, and went for them instead. The breeder had offered them two for the price of one (kinda), and off home they went with two of the world's most powerful and potentially intimidating dogs, when all they really wanted was something fluffy that looked cute! Of course, looks are important and we all want to spend our lives looking at things that please our eye but, as my friends with the Akitas learned, looks really aren't everything.

A pal

Companionship, of course, is the biggest answer. People say they want a dog for the company. And dogs do, on the whole, make great companions (although you shouldn't always bank on bringing home the kind of best buddy you see depicted on TV shows and in books. Not all dogs are Lassie or Timmy from the Famous Five, some prefer their own company far more than you might expect). It's not for nothing that we call them man's – or woman's – best friend. I'm all for this being the reason that you want a puppy. But here's the catch: like any relationship, for it to work, it has got to be a two-way thing.

As far as I'm aware, no one has ever asked any puppies what they want from a new owner (at least if they did, the answer wasn't forthcoming), but as someone who has worked with them for donkey's years, I can tell you that any successful puppy and parent partnership is exactly that – a partnership. If you've got lots of love to give and you want to shower your puppy with affection that's great, but simply lavishing them with cuddles and treats when you have the time will usually result in an adult dog who is confused about their boundaries and can find it difficult to function in the adult, human world.

As well as loving them, you need to take the time to understand what your puppy really needs, to understand why they do the things they do, and to have the courage to hold your ground even when their puppy-dog eyes try to make you do otherwise (don't underestimate the irresistible power of puppy-dog eyes, they're a force of nature!). You've got to be prepared to be there for your puppy through thick and thin, not only to love them, but also to guide them and provide for them, despite the chewed-up sofa leg and weed-on cushions that will almost certainly happen in those first few weeks and months. In return they'll give you their love, loyalty, and all the fun and exercise you can ask for. But it has always got to be a two-way street.

HOW DO PUPPIES LOOK SO CUTE?

Humans have fallen prey to the cuteness overload of puppies ever since we first domesticated their wolf ancestors over 30,000 years ago. But how did they manage to perfect that doleful, imploring look, that makes us go so weak at the knees?

In 2019, scientists at the University of Plymouth's Centre for Comparative and Evolutionary Psychology conducted research in partnership with universities from Pittsburgh, Raleigh and Washington in the US, and discovered that dogs have gradually developed a new forehead muscle – the *levator anguli oculi medialis* – that wolves do not have. This muscle allows them to be able to raise their eyebrows more intensely, which creates an expression that makes them look younger and more vulnerable. Researchers studied old taxidermy models of dogs and wolves, and found that all dogs, except for the wolf-like Siberian husky, have this muscle.

The team hypothesised that dogs' expressive eyebrows provoke a nurturing response in humans and evolved to become a dominant feature as a result of selection based on humans' preferences. Or, to put it more simply, we have bred the cute factor into our dogs, because it speaks to our instinct to look after something or someone. Pretty cool, eh?

Hopefully I haven't put you off and you've now thought hard about exactly why you want a puppy, and you feel ready to embrace the challenge that lies ahead. Good for you! So, once you know why you want one, the next thing you need to think about is what kind of puppy is right for you.

🐾 *REMEMBER!* No two dogs will ever be the same. If you grew up with a brilliant Irish setter who was the most wonderful and best-behaved animal ever (unlikely, if it was a setter, but you get where I'm going with this), that doesn't automatically mean you're going to get the same dog again. You might not even get a dog who is remotely similar. We'll talk more about breeds and temperaments as we go on, but for now just bear in mind that each dog has its own unique personality. And, for the purposes of choosing a puppy, you should try to remove any rose-tinted spectacles you might be wearing when thinking about that lovely dog you had in childhood, dogs who seem good fun in TV shows, or a dog you met once who seemed like a nice bloke.

Dog Breed Characteristics and Their Origins

If you've ever watched Crufts you'll know that in the UK, and pretty much the rest of the world, we tend to categorise dogs based on the groups established by the Kennel Club. These categories were created over a hundred years ago, to help regulate the burgeoning popularity of showing dogs and field trials, and to keep for the first time, records for breeding purposes. Here's a quick rundown of the Kennel Club categories and their origins:

Hounds
From dachshunds and bassets to borzois and Irish wolfhounds, these dogs were originally bred to help humans to hunt, either with their incredible eyesight or powerful sense of smell.

Gundogs
Setters, retrievers, pointers and spaniels were all bred to help aristocrats and their staff when out shooting birds. They were good at flushing out prey, alerting the hunters to targets, and with their soft mouths, picking up and returning the kill.

Terriers
From Yorkshires and Westies to Jack Russells and Airedales, terriers were bred to find and kill rats, moles and other vermin. They are spirited, characterful dogs and generally smaller than many working or gundogs, so are a popular choice for smaller homes.

Utility

This group includes dogs like Dalmatians, poodles and the fashionable French bulldog, all of them bred with very specific purposes, often related to their location or the class of their owners. Dalmatians, for example, were bred to run alongside carriages while French bulldogs were the adopted mascot of avant-garde Parisians at the turn of the nineteenth century.

Working

Working dogs have been bred to help human beings in their jobs, whether it's guarding flocks, working with the police or as mountain rescue dogs. They can be small or enormous, and as a group their temperaments are all very different. The one thing they have in common are their strong natural instincts, which owners need to be aware of and work with.

Pastoral

Pastoral dogs have been bred to herd livestock. In the UK that usually means sheep but there are pastoral dogs all over the world herding all sorts of flocks, from lamas to cattle and even reindeer. They are usually very bright and helpful, and like having a job to do, so they make great family pets – but they do also need plenty of exercise.

Toy dogs

Bichon frise, Maltese, pugs and Chihuahuas are all popular examples of toy dogs. Toys come in many shapes but only one size: small. They have been bred mostly for companionship and despite being quite tiny they can have big personalities.

Fascinating stuff. And of course, many of the characteristics and natural instincts that dogs were bred for are still an innate part of their temperaments today. We'll look more closely at these 'breed standards' shortly (see page 21). But unless you are a gamekeeper or someone who works with dogs every day, or unless you want to breed and show them at Crufts, these categories can seem fairly meaningless to the average modern family, or person, who is looking for a pet.

Graeme's Puppy-Choosing Process Flow Chart

Knowing that all dogs have unique character traits and how some are better suited to certain environments, I always like to get people to think about the kind of puppy they would be best suited to by using a sort of mental process flow chart (although, it doesn't need to be mental, you can also write it down!).

It's a super-simple process but one that often surprises people because some of the things you might expect to be most important, like size and looks for example, are not actually the first things to consider. Let's take a closer look.

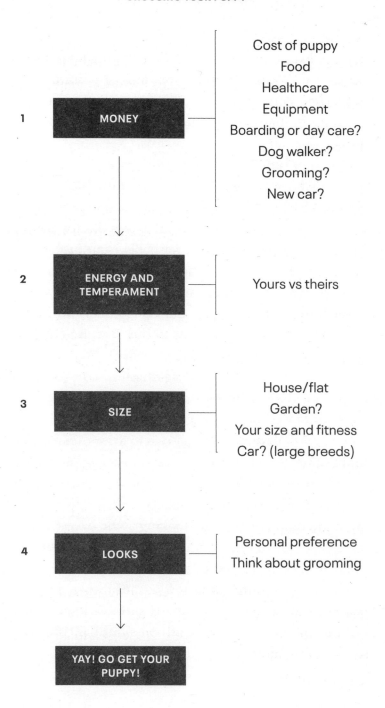

1 MONEY
- Cost of puppy
- Food
- Healthcare
- Equipment
- Boarding or day care?
- Dog walker?
- Grooming?
- New car?

2 ENERGY AND TEMPERAMENT
- Yours vs theirs

3 SIZE
- House/flat
- Garden?
- Your size and fitness
- Car? (large breeds)

4 LOOKS
- Personal preference
- Think about grooming

YAY! GO GET YOUR PUPPY!

Money

No one likes to think about this one, but giving it some thought now may save you thousands of pounds in the long run. Puppies cost money, dogs cost even more money over their lifetime, and some dogs cost a lot more money than others.

I'm not only talking about the price you pay to buy one, which for a typical Labrador in the UK can start at around £1,000, and for more exotic or fashionable breeds can go up to crazy numbers. But the cost of feeding them, keeping them healthy, vets' bills, insurance, kitting them out, taking them on holiday (or leaving them with kennels/sitters), walking services and all the myriad other things that you are required to cough up for. It's not only how much they cost to buy, but the cost over their lifetime that you need to consider.

You might imagine that big dogs will cost you more than little dogs, and that is true to some extent. Your Newfoundland may eat five times as much food, need larger beds and require bigger cars to drive them around in, but they are likely to live a far shorter life than your scruffy cross-breed terrier, who probably doesn't eat that much, but will live to a ripe old age.

Sometimes, rather than looking at the overall cost of a dog, it helps to think about the affordability. Much in the same way that you would with a mortgage, considering whether the monthly costs – food, insurance, petrol if you need to drive to your walking spot – are something you can afford right now, month on month, is crucial for selecting the most suitable dog.

◐ *TIP:* One thing that will always cost you more with a bigger (or heavier) dog is medicine, the doses of which are related to a dog's bodyweight. Whereas two humans of different sizes could both take the same amount of paracetamol for a headache, a mastiff and a Chihuahua could have the same problem and be prescribed the same medication, but it will be given in different quantities and the price will vary. Something worth thinking about when working out the affordability of your puppy.

Energy and temperament

This all sounds very spiritual for a Yorkshireman, I know. But bear with me. I want you to think first about the kind of energy you want from your puppy. By which I mean both physical energy and the kind of energy they give off (I told you it was a bit spiritual). Also, think about the kind of energy that you have. Make sure that you consider what kind of energy complements your energy. Really think about it. Do you want a dog full of vim and vigour who is always ready to go go go, or a peaceful, serene animal who likes to lounge around all day? A dog who'll make you feel protected or one who needs reassurance in social situations? Soppy? Noble? There are lots of qualities to think about. I don't usually condone the anthropomorphisation of canines, but in this case, I find it's useful to think about the kind of person you are and the kind of people you tend to feel happiest around, the kind of personality you can make space for in your life. This, more than anything, will not only help you narrow down your choice of puppy, but make sure your relationship with that puppy stays the distance.

🐾 *REMEMBER!* You're not necessarily looking for a match here. If you've got a super-bouncy, active dog who needs loads of attention and you're also really busy doing things all day, this may not be a wise pairing. Opposites do attract, after all.

Size

Yes, the rumours are true: size matters! Once you have worked out what kind of dog you want around the place, and how much you can afford to spend on it, you're going to have to think about what size dog you're going to be raising.

It doesn't matter how much you love the look of a glorious Great Dane, and how much you have always wanted their slobber in vertical stripes up your walls. And how much you imagine you will enjoy forevermore people pointing and saying, 'You could put a saddle on that!' Simply put, if you are living in a one-bed flat on the sixth floor in the town centre, it's probably not the best breed for you to choose. Clearly, that's an extreme example, but you get my point. You need to think about where you live and, if you have got easy access to outdoor space, how much is there. How big is your car? How big (and fit) are you? Cut your coat according to your cloth, as the old saying goes. (Funny how it doesn't really work the other way around. A small dog in a big house isn't such a problem, is it? Unless you're worried about losing them, I suppose. I'm aware of at least one lady with a very large house in London who kept corgis and never seemed to have any trouble finding them.)

Has considering the size of your potential dog taken any other breeds off the list?

Looks

Finally – and I really do mean finally – do you like the look of them? (Although I know you're thinking, who am I, in my waistcoat and cravat, to suggest looks don't matter?) You're going to spend a long time looking at each other, this puppy and you. They're stuck with your ugly fizzog, but we humans do get a choice, so use it wisely. Do you really love the squashed-up face of a pug and will you still love it in ten years when it's all grey and grizzled and possibly covered in lumps? The refined grace and (high-maintenance!) long locks of a regal Afghan hound are undoubtedly beautiful, but could this be infatuation and might your head be turned by a cheeky boxer one day soon? There's no right or wrong here, you'll know when you know.

Finding the Perfect Breeder

Now, hopefully you've whittled down your shortlist to one or two possible breed options. The next thing you need to do is work out where and how to find one. I always think it's a bit like buying a second-hand car, there are so many different options and dealers out there, it's hard to know where to start and who to trust. Do you buy online? Find a breeder through word of mouth? How do you know you're getting a healthy dog? What's a puppy farm? How can you avoid them? How old should the puppy be? Should you get a rescue dog? It's enough to make you throw in the towel before you've begun.

Never fear! I've got all the information you need to make sure you find the right puppy.

A word about impulse buying

Before we get into the nitty-gritty of going for it, I just want to flag up the problem of impulse buying. I have lost track of how many people have told me they bought a puppy on impulse. Maybe they just went to see the puppies and before they knew it, they'd brought one home, or their friend got one so they rushed out and got one too. I truly know how enticing a puppy can be and I understand how easy it is to find yourself with one in your pocket before you know it! But I urge you to take a moment, step back and sit with the feeling.

I grew up in Selby, which is – hands-down – North Yorkshire's premier market town (ahem). There was a man called Howard who sold crockery on the market every Monday. He was a showman, one of the old-school salespeople who always managed to gather a huge crowd around him as he sold his cheap-as-chips plates and bowls and mugs. Howard was as smart as he was entertaining. He knew exactly how to create a sales frenzy. 'These are the last ones I can get hold of and I've only got three sets left,' he'd shout. You could hear him a mile off. 'Go to Marks and Sparks, ladies, and they'll cost you fifty quid. I don't want that. I don't even want twenty. No! For the first three people who hand me the cash, you can take them away today for a tenner. A tenner. I must be mad! Who's first?!' If you think Usain Bolt is quick, you've never seen how fast a crockery-crazed Selby housewife could move in the days before Amazon was invented. It was breathtaking.

I sometimes feel that, intentionally or otherwise, we go into Selby market mode when looking for a puppy. We become one of Howard's desperate customers: we want that puppy and we want it NOW!

I want to remind you that just as Howard could always get more tableware from his van out the back, there will always be more puppies to choose from. It is better for you, and the puppies, that you wait and know that you are absolutely ready, rather than take one on before the time is right.

◖ *TIP:* Use my six-month rule. When you think you can't possibly live without a puppy any longer, write it down in a notebook or diary. Now put the book away and make a note to come back to it in six months (yes, six whole months). If you can say, hand on heart, that you still want a puppy, then crack on!

Your puppy's age

One of the first things you need to consider is how old your puppy should be when you bring it home. Experts tend to agree that around the eight-week mark is the best time to separate a puppy from its litter. Why? Because any earlier and they may miss out on vital nutrition from their mother's milk and interaction with mum and their littermates, but much later and your puppy will be missing out on experiences which happen outside the litter. In other words, eight weeks is a great time to start the socialisation process (see Chapter 4 for more on this), as your puppy's internal record button is set to 'on' for a limited time. The clock is ticking for their young brains to absorb all the information they need to live a happy life.

◖ *TIP:* If you're not sure how old your puppy is or you're worried that you might be buying a pup who has been taken away too early from their mum, it could be worth acquainting yourself with what an eight-week-old puppy of your chosen breed looks like.

Just look at the way a puppy changes in those first eight weeks:

WEEKS 1 - 2: Newborn is fully dependent on mum. Limited mobility. Touch and taste senses only. Can't see, hear or manage body temperature yet. Sleeps and eats. Eyes and ears open at 2 weeks.

WEEKS 3 - 4: Puppy begins to learn about surroundings and show curiosity. Learns to vocalise, crawl and stand, taking wobbly steps by 3 weeks.

WEEKS 5 - 6: Interaction with littermates, mother and humans. Developing walking, possibly barking, wagging tail. Vision fully develops at 5 weeks.

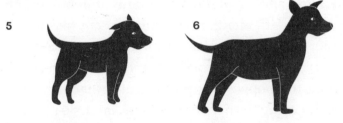

WEEKS 7 - 8: We might introduce first collar and lead. Begin learning fun recall. Our puppy is consuming solid foods at 8 weeks. First fear period. Also a playful phase.

And if you are reading this and have just arrived home with your 12-week-old puppy, please do not shriek and immediately take it back to the breeder! The eight-week mark is a guideline and bringing home a puppy who is older than this, is not the end of the world by any means. As we'll learn as we go through this book, raising a puppy is about the constant ebb and flow of nature and nurture. Nothing is ever perfect. However old they are when they come into your care and whatever their nature, there is always a nurturing response to be made.

Breeders and what to know

Most puppies come from the pairing of two dogs who have been 'bred' by their owners, aka breeders. Forgive me if that seems pretty obvious. What's perhaps not so obvious is that you don't need any qualifications to breed dogs and anyone who owns a dog is at liberty to breed their dog with another one and let them have puppies if they so wish. Once you start doing it regularly (in the UK it's three litters or more in a 12-month period) and selling the puppies for profit, that's when you need a dog breeding licence. But because most dog breeding takes place in people's homes, behind closed doors, it's notoriously difficult to regulate and monitor breeding practices. And as customers, it's sometimes difficult to know if you are dealing with a legitimate breeder or not.

I've got some tips to help you navigate the process of finding and dealing with breeders, most of whom are genuine dog lovers, it must be said. But first, let's just have a look at how the kind of puppy you are buying can affect the process.

Buying a pedigree puppy

What does 'pedigree' actually mean? It's a way of describing a dog who has been bred from two dogs of the same breed, by a Kennel Club-registered breeder, and its birth recognised and recorded by the Kennel Club. (You'll also hear people talk about 'pure breeds', these are dogs of the same breed but not necessarily registered with the Kennel Club.) There is, of course, an argument that all pedigrees and pure breeds are essentially mixed breeds. They've all been selectively bred over the years to achieve the 'standards' we judge them by now. You only need to look at some of the dogs in paintings in the National Gallery to see how the features of certain dogs have been altered over time by selective breeding.

If you've decided on a pedigree breed, your first port of call should be the Kennel Club, where you'll find thousands of pedigree breeders listed. Good pedigree breeders are professionals, who have high standards of care and welfare and may have had, or still have, prize-winning dogs in their care. I have a huge amount of respect for good professional breeders, they have a genuine talent for mixing bloodlines and creating dogs who don't only look fantastic but are healthy and strong with flawless temperaments. I'm no geneticist, but I think of breeding puppies as a bit like baking a cake. Once it's baked, it's baked, so you really need to know what you are doing with the ingredients. The good pedigree breeders are the Michelin-star chefs!

However, and this is where it gets complicated, a Kennel Club registration doesn't automatically guarantee a breeder will be prioritising health and temperament over appearance. Many do, but not all. Unfortunately, some less-than-perfect breeders use it as a marketing tool to give themselves credibility. Conversely, you can also buy a pure breed from a breeder who is not registered with the Kennel Club, but who may also be a wonderful and responsible breeder producing great dogs. I told you it was confusing! Just remember to prioritise health and temperament over appearance.

Buying a cross-breed puppy

What about a cross-breed dog? A cross-breed dog is, as the name suggests, the result of breeding two dogs of different breeds. Again, the idea of creating a power-combo of two breeds isn't a new thing. For as long as I can remember, we've had lurchers (a common mix of sighthound and a working breed, usually a terrier or collie) and there are a number of much-loved terriers, like Patterdale terriers and Jack Russells, which are not recognised as 'pedigree' dogs by the Kennel Club but endure as breeds in the collective consciousness, nonetheless. To put it another way, dogs have been cross-breeding quite happily for centuries.

Over the past 20 years or so we've seen a huge surge in the popularity of so-called designer dogs, cross-breeds such as cockerpoos, labradoodles, cavapoochons and almost any other combinations of popular dogs you can think of. Their names seem to get ever more bonkers (did someone order a peekapoo or a sproodle?) and the promises of what they can offer ever more spurious (there is, just for the record, no such thing as a truly hypo-allergenic dog). And for the most part, these cross-breed dogs are fantastic! But cross-breeding capers can also put you and the puppies at risk of dealing with unscrupulous people, who are keen to cash in on the demand for designer dogs without paying due care to the genetics involved. Furthermore, with unregulated, inexpert breeding comes the greater risk of health and behaviour problems.

THE LEGEND OF THE HYPO-ALLERGENIC DOG

You hear a lot of talk about how some dogs have been bred to be hypo-allergenic, because they don't shed their fur. While it's true that some dogs shed less fur than others, the idea that they are somehow hypo-allergenic is unfortunately not true. Most of the sources that cause allergies to dogs are found within the proteins of their saliva and wee. The proteins stick to the dogs' fur and skin, so if you have a low-shed dog, you're less likely to come into contact with the proteins that cause your allergies to flare up. The bottom line is, if you are worried about allergies, don't get a big shaggy dog that slobbers everywhere!

That is not to say that all the cross-breeds you come across will face issues, far from it: intelligent cross-breeding can create hybrid vigour, a tendency for cross-bred animals to be fitter and healthier than their parents. The problem is it is something of a Wild West out there! Luckily a lot of these popular cross-breeds now have regulatory bodies of their own, which operate in a similar way to the Kennel Club. For example, there is the British Cockerpoo Society and the Labradoodle Association of the UK. These groups are run by enthusiasts and experts who love and understand the breed, and often list breeders in your local area in the same way that the Kennel Club does, so always worth checking in with these organisations before you start looking.

Red flags and warning signs

Whether you are opting for a pedigree showstopper, a designer cross-breed or are happy to consider any kind of cross, there are some basic signs and red flags to look out for. Bear these tips in mind when you are looking for and talking to breeders:

- Can you see the puppies with their mother? Like babies, puppies need to go through a natural process of growth and development in the first few weeks and months and rely on their mother's milk for all their nourishment. If puppies have been taken away from their mother too soon it can be a sign of maltreatment.

- Look at the environment the dogs are in. Is there clear evidence that the puppies are being looked after? Is there general evidence that the breeder cares? Go with your gut instincts. If it looks dodgy or doesn't feel right, it probably isn't.

- How experienced is the breeder? Is this their first rodeo? Don't be afraid to ask questions about the dam (the mother) and how many litters she has had. There's no right answer but the breeder should ideally be happy to tell you and share the information with you.

- Is the breeder interested in you and your home? Are they asking you as many questions as you are asking them? A good breeder will care about where their dogs are ending up. Did it feel like a grilling? Good!

- If the breeder has a website, what does it tell you about them? If there is a lot of boasting about how many prizes they won at Crufts, I'm not necessarily impressed! If they want to tell you all about their puppies' temperament and suitability as pets, and how they have selectively bred to avoid common health problems with the breed, then keep reading!

A BAD EXAMPLE OF A BREEDER

A friend made an enquiry via a Kennel Club-registered breeder's website about a new litter of German short-haired pointer puppies that were soon to be available. Assuming it wouldn't be an automatic process, she emailed the breeder asking how she could register her interest for one of the puppies. The reply came five minutes later, saying there were two puppies left, a boy and a girl, and they would take a £500 deposit now, with £1,500 to pay on collection.

My friend felt instantly that this didn't sound like a particularly responsible breeder. They hadn't asked her any questions about where the dog would live, or if she had any experience with the breed, and they had gone straight to money. As tempting as it was to simply ping over the money and guarantee herself the puppy she was looking for, she also knew that the breeder's lack of care could point to problems with the pup further down the line.

TIP: If you are able to get to know a breeder – perhaps via a contact or just a few chats on the phone – and you feel you trust them and their instincts, consider inviting them to choose the best puppy for you. As I said earlier, a good breeder really is an expert and will know which of the litter is right for your home and lifestyle.

Recognising puppy farms

Puppy farms sound almost idyllic, don't they? You might imagine green fields full of frolicking puppies and wonder what all the fuss about them is. Unfortunately, they are more like factory farms than the farms of children's stories, with female dogs being kept in a state of near constant pregnancy and distress, as their owners force them to reproduce at maximum levels for maximum profit. Puppies are often taken away from their mothers too early and may suffer ill health (and can sometimes die) as a result of being removed too soon. The conditions are usually dirty and, because puppy farmers are often trying to hide what they are doing, can lack light and ventilation.

Because of the poor conditions, puppy farmers sometimes use third-party sellers, who pretend to be the breeder, and instead of inviting you to see the puppies at home with their mum, they might offer to bring you the puppy instead, or ask to meet you at a location (service stations seems to be a favourite). They may also advertise the puppies online and sell you the puppy straight away, without any discussion.

And the more popular the breed you're looking for, the higher likelihood you'll come across dogs who are the result of puppy farming. In 2021, the RSPCA reported a staggering 1,571 per cent increase in the number of French bulldogs going into its care over the year, as owners who had bought the fashionable pups during lockdown struggled with the complications and expenses caused by poor breeding in puppy farms. The RSPCA also reported increased numbers of cockerpoos and other cocker crosses, as well as Chihuahuas and Chihuahua-crosses, all of them fashionable breeds.

It is so hard to walk away from a puppy you suspect has come from a farm, but I urge you to resist the temptation to 'rescue' a dog from this situation. Instead, if you think you have seen anything that looks like animal abuse or a breach of welfare laws, walk away and report any concerns you may have to your local RSPCA. It is incredibly hard for the authorities to detect these operations, and it is only by receiving tip-offs and information that they are able to stop them operating.

Visually- and hearing-impaired dogs

All I want to say here is this: don't rule out a dog who is deaf or blind. Many people imagine a dog with a disability is only for the most experienced owners, and I'm not suggesting it's something you should take on lightly. But in some ways, a dog with impaired vision or hearing can make a brilliant first dog. Let me explain why.

I once went to see a woman who had taken on a blind puppy – the irony was it had been bred for the Guide Dogs for the Blind, but once they realised he was blind, he was withdrawn for rehoming. The owner hadn't had a dog before and wanted me to help teach her the basics, starting with walking on the lead. We both imagined the dog would struggle to know which direction to walk in and would probably need some extra voice commands to stay on track. So, I took the little chap outside in the garden with the lead on and began to walk up and down, using my voice to keep him aware of where I was and let him know if I was going to turn left or right. I noticed immediately that the lead almost never got tight, he didn't pull or veer off in the wrong direction or get distracted by an interesting smell, like any other puppy might do. He stayed by my side all the time. I thought this was interesting so I dropped the voice commands to see if he would stay by my side without them, and he did. Then I took the lead off him completely and just walked up and down and around the garden, and the little guy stuck with me every step of the way. He didn't need especially complicated training, he knew where he needed to be. No one present was more surprised than me by what this puppy could do, and therein lies a lesson: focusing on what a disabled dog is capable of, rather than getting bogged down with their limitations, is always the way to go.

We still know so little about the canine brain and their incredibly powerful senses. I wouldn't be surprised to hear that they have other senses that we haven't discovered yet. This little puppy was almost magnetic. I'll never forget him.

But the point I'm trying to make is this: blind or deaf dogs can be extremely adaptable and can make wonderful pets. Amputee dogs too. Their owners often develop incredibly strong bonds with them because of the symbiotic relationship that develops. They all need a home – could it be yours?

Puppies from rescue homes

People tend to think of rescue dogs as adult dogs, but puppies often need rescuing too! Pregnant dogs are especially common in rescue homes, as people can't cope with the prospect of a litter on the way and give the dogs up before the puppies come. Even if they haven't been born at the rescue home and are a little older than the optimum eight weeks for taking home, they are puppies and they still need a home!

The benefits of a rescue puppy don't stop at knowing you're doing a good thing. They will usually come with all the appropriate paperwork and vaccinations, and won't have the price tag of a dog from a private breeder.

You'll usually need to fill out a few forms and an inspector may wish to visit your home before the puppy comes back with you. You might also be invited to spend some time with your new pup at the centre, to get them used to your smell and check for any potential allergies you might have.

It's a very considered and responsible approach to taking on a puppy, and by the time you open the door and bring them home, you will really be sure that you want them to be there. The message here is: give rescue puppies your full consideration!

So, you've really been honest with yourself about whether you can look after a puppy, and you've asked yourself some big questions about the kind of dog you think will be right for you and your home. Before you come to any final decisions, double-check you've been through these key points.

Key Points

- Think about the kind of dog you want in your life, not what it will look like or how funny it will be.

- Research, research, research – take your time!

- Be puppy farm-aware, ask for licences and go through official channels where possible.

- Consider rescue and disabled puppies.

- Be sure that you can afford it!

Next Step

Time to start getting ready
for your new arrival!

NOTES

Chapter 2

Getting Ready for Your Puppy

Making all the puppy preparations you need for a smooth transition

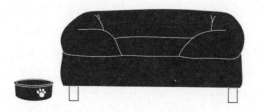

I regularly hear from people who have gone to see some puppies down the road or at a friend's house, with no intention whatsoever of getting one at all – they swear they just want a cuddle – only to find an hour later that they've come home with a dog in the shopping basket from the boot of the car and have absolutely nothing in the house that a puppy needs. Their messages usually start with, 'Help! What do I do now?!'

Hopefully, if you are reading this, you're NOT one of those people and you have arrived at this point after some very careful consideration and research. (But if you are one of those people, please don't worry – you can keep reading from here and everything will be fine.)

Puppies are quite simple creatures and only need a few things in place to stay happy and contented during the first few hours and days at their new home. Being ready for their arrival will help them, but it will also help you feel calm and in control, or at least mildly on top of things, when this little bundle of chaos and joy enters your life.

In a moment we'll start writing that puppy shopping list but first things first – this puppy is going to need a name!

What's in a Name?

What will you call your puppy? Choosing a name is all part of the fun, and the kind of thing you can lose hours thinking about and discussing with the family – mostly because it's something everyone in your family is likely to have an opinion about.

As you can imagine, I meet puppies with all sorts of funny names. I think my favourite has to be the guy whose black Labrador was called Taxi. It wasn't only because 'black Lab' sounds a bit like 'black cab', but more because he liked the idea of standing in a field in the middle of the countryside, shouting 'Taxiiiii!'

(Puppy naming rule number one: if you're going to give them a joke name, make sure the joke is still going to be funny after you've said it 8,000 times. I've met a few dogs called Deefur, as in 'D fer Dog'. It was a fad a few years ago and everyone who named a puppy Deefur seemed to think they were the only one. If it's not going to have you and everyone you meet chuckling 12 years down the line, you might want to reconsider. In all fairness, it was quite funny the first time I heard it.)

Joking aside, Taxi isn't actually a bad name to give

your dog and I'll tell you why: it's got two strong syllables. Names with two syllables are good in my book (that'll be this book, then), because they are usually clear sounds that can't be easily confused with other words. Not much sounds like or rhymes with taxi. (You're going through a mental checklist of words that might rhyme right now, aren't you?)

Most of the commands you'll soon be teaching your puppy will be audible, so the less confusion there is for them about what a sound means, the better. They'll also mostly be one syllable, words like *STAY* and *DOWN*. So, by all means call your puppy Faye or Neil, but be prepared for some possible mix-ups, when it comes to training time.

Taxi, despite its comedic origins, is a phonetically clear word that a dog can easily recognise and respond to, even when they are very busy sniffing everything in the garden or chasing next door's cat. I've never met another dog called Taxi since.

Should you call your dog by a human name? People are often divided over this, with many folks feeling it is a kind of disrespectful anthropomorphisation to call a big hairy beast with four legs Emily. My take on this is that most of us are clever enough to know that Gordon here is a Rottweiler, not a human, and in the end, names are simply sounds that help animals and other human beings know that you are talking to them – labels, so to speak. If you really start to go down this ideological path, you might come to the conclusion that you shouldn't give a dog a name at all, and only talk to them in sign language or grunts (which is not entirely impossible, but a subject for a different book).

Some people delegate the responsibility of choosing a puppy name to their children. I've certainly met a few Disney-inspired Jasmines and Elsas over the years. I don't object to this in principle, but I offer a word of caution in that you can risk breaking someone's heart if the name they decide on is one you simply cannot live with. I met a little lad who wanted to call his new puppy Xbox and, quite rightly, his mum put her foot down about it. Thankfully he was a good-natured soul who took the rejection on the chin, but other children might not always be so ready to accept defeat. Children also grow out of their passions, so while Lightning McQueen might be where it's at when the puppy arrives, fast forward a few years and your grumpy goth teenager might not enjoy being reminded of his former *Cars*-crazy self. I guess the moral of the story here is that a family decision is probably a wiser move than handing over sole responsibility to a five-year-old.

And on the subject of children, it's a good idea to choose a name that is distinct from the other names you might be shouting out a lot over the years. If your kids are called Flo and Beau, calling your dog Joe might not turn out to be very helpful.

The other important thing to remember about the name you choose is that your vet will use it very often with your surname when they call your dog in for appointments. So, it can be worth thinking of something that works with your family name. My surname's Hall, so a dog called Bea, for example, might cause confusion in the waiting room when the vet calls out, 'Be all!' (And who among us could resist shouting 'End all!' in response?) It could be worse. I once saw a builder's van in Hull with the legend F. Hall & Son writ large on the side. I digress …

Naming a rescue puppy

Puppies from a rescue centre will have a name already when you meet them. Different centres have different systems for naming animals, some go by the alphabet so that a whole litter might have names beginning with D, others go by theme, so you might have a litter named after characters from a soap opera. However they come to have the name they have, in an ideal world it is best to keep the same name. This makes the transition from rescue centre to your home less confusing for the dog, and it keeps your paperwork simpler!

But, of course, if you want to change the name you can! It's not the end of the world and is easy enough to put into effect. If you can change it to something that sounds similar to the existing name, that's nice and easy. If Tyson is to become Bryson, simply keep saying Bryson until everyone has forgotten about Tyson. If it's a bigger change in sounds and syllables, say Tyson is going to become Barney, then it is a simple case of saying the new name to the puppy and rewarding them with a treat as and when they respond. Your puppy will begin to associate their new name with nice things and eventually their old name will become a thing of the past.

GETTING READY FOR YOUR PUPPY

Getting the House Puppy-Ready

Hopefully now you've decided on a name for your new family member and so it's time to get the house ready and pick up a few essentials before the big arrival!

Puppy-proofing your home

INSIDE

So much of what you'll need to do will depend on your space and how it's used. But there are some immovable facts about the small tornado you are about to let off in your home that need to be handled wherever you live.

Puppies wee ... a lot. They also love to explore (see: escape) and they use their teeth to find out about the world. With these three points in mind, it is wise to get your home puppy-ready for the invasion.

Ideally, until they can understand life a little better, you'll want to keep them away from rooms with nice furniture and carpets in, easy access to harsh chemicals such as bleach, and anything else that can harm them, or you, such as batteries, electrical wiring or sharp objects, and/or anything they can get stuck inside of, like washing machines and ovens. (However unlikely it seems, sadly it happens!)

For lots of folk, this will mean keeping a new puppy mostly confined to one or two safe areas in the house – the kitchen and utility room are most common – but also making sure cupboards are closed and not easily opened (it's handy if you also have young children and can fit the cupboards with child locks).

If you don't want to have your internal doors closed to create these puppy rooms, a gate or two will help you create the space you need without shutting off the rooms entirely.

OUTSIDE

If you have a garden, there are three important things to consider. Firstly, make sure that getting into the garden is relatively quick and easy for them. If the path to the back door resembles an assault course to you, imagine what it looks like to a puppy! It really is worth spending some time to clear the way, so that your excited puppy can get to the grass when they need a wee, and so that you can respond quickly to any signals they might give you (more on toilet training on page 146). You'll also want to avoid impact on their growing and relatively delicate joints, which can lead to long-term damage, so think carefully about how to avoid them jumping down from high steps and garden walls. The same applies inside. Don't let your puppy run down the stairs.

The other thing you want to be sure of is that your puppy can't escape from the garden. This is easier if you have a walled garden but if you have hedges, which they can squeeze through, and/or fences that they can dig under, it is very important that you secure the garden before they arrive. Puppies are incurably curious, stupendously brave and lightning-quick, and will not think twice about pushing themselves through the tiniest hole to investigate an interesting smell in next door's garden. Before you know it, they can be in the road and you have a tragedy on your hands. If there is any doubt in your mind about the security of your garden, keep them on a lead when you're outside with them – and get busy with that chicken wire!

Finally, have a good hard look at the plants in your garden. Your puppy is bound to get their chops around most of them sooner or later, but it's important to know that some of them may be poisonous – to dogs, if not humans. I'm good with dogs but famously rubbish with plants. Have a search online for a list, and if you aren't sure what's in your garden, perhaps it's time to call a green-fingered friend.

Crate expectations

One of the first things you'll need to think about getting hold of is a crate. A lot of people don't like the idea of a puppy crate and I can see why. It's basically a metal cage that you have to plonk in your kitchen, or wherever you decide to have it. And cages – all hard edges and involuntary captivity – are absolutely the opposite of what most of us want for our puppy, which is lots of cuddles, fun and love. And when you have spent a lot of time and energy making your house just-so, it can be galling to have to try to live with a cage in the middle of it.

I'm not vehemently opposed to crates, but I'm not all for them either. I think to a large extent it depends on the dog and your situation. If they have been used to a crate at their first home, it is probably a good idea to continue with a crate at home. If they've been used to running around in wide open space, and you have plenty of safe space at home, it might not be worth trying to get them used to a crate and could even be traumatising for them. I'm not going to tell you that you absolutely should get a crate; however, they can have some advantages – mostly for the puppy, one or two for you.

So, what are the benefits of a puppy crate? Well, before we even discuss the benefits, the first thing you need to remember is that a puppy doesn't know it's a crate or a cage. So, all the negative associations you might have with such a contraption don't apply to the puppy.

The other thing to remember is that you will – ideally – pad the crate out with some nice soft blankets and a couple of reassuring toys, so that it's actually a cosy little den where a puppy can retreat for some peace and quiet when life gets overwhelming, and not the stark metal cage you might think it is.

It's also somewhere safe for you to keep your puppy if you need to – maybe you have the plumber coming or need to have the front door open to unpack the shopping. A crate will give you peace of mind that your little pup is safe while you do what you need to do.

A crate is NOT somewhere your puppy should be spending hours on end in. We'll come to how to use your crate and get your puppy used to it in the next chapter. For now, have a think about whether it is right for you.

WHAT TO PUT IN YOUR CRATE

Back in my early days of dog training we had a thing called newspaper, which we used to line the bottom of crates. Some of my older readers might remember newspaper! We used that, and a few old blankets that could be washed when the puppy had weed on them. These days, no one reads the news on paper anymore and what with smart phones not being very absorbent, we are lucky to have something called vet bedding. This is a product that I think is essential for any new puppy at home. As the name suggests, vet bedding is used by vets when treating animals in their surgeries and hospitals. It's now widely available to consumers as well. It's a specially made double-strength polyester fabric, with super-dense fibres, which makes it soft and warm for animals to lie on, while also being highly permeable so air can flow through it. The best bit about this material, though, is that it allows for drainage, so if and when a puppy has a little accident on the bedding, the moisture drains through and they're not left sitting in a soggy, smelly blanket for you to wash.

Line the bottom of your crate with vet bedding, then simply empty the tray in the bottom of your crate and give it a wash down whenever your puppy has a tinkle in there.

A couple of old blankets are also good for going over the top and sides of the crate. This will keep it warm and dark in there – puppy heaven for when they need 40 winks.

WHERE DO YOU BUY A CRATE?

Check eBay and other local selling sites for second-hand crates rather than buying new. They are quite readily available because people tend not to keep them for the dog's entire life. Also, try to look for a crate with a handle on top – this makes it easy to move and transport smaller puppies when you're off to the vet or on a long journey.

HOW CAN I CREATE A SAFE SPACE
WITHOUT A CRATE?

If you don't want to buy a metal crate, consider how you can create a 'safe space' at home, maybe with a child's stair gate (that is no longer in use!) to cordon off a small corner, or an area under the worksurface where your puppy can cosy up when they are tired. Think safe and warm, rather than wide-open space.

TIP: There are some incredibly fancy crates available to buy these days, with tasteful drapes and designer cushions to match your living room. The Yorkshireman in me objects to spending a lot of money on something like this, but the man on the telly who wears a cravat does understand that sometimes you want things to look the way you like them. To save money, instead of spending fortunes on a pre-accessorised crate, you could try approaching it as a design project and jazz it up with second-hand blankets in the colours you like. I've seen people put fairy lights around them and dress them up with tinsel at Christmas and all sorts – I don't recommend you do either of these things for a very young puppy because of the chewing and choking risks.

What about a bed?

Some people have a crate, others have an open dog bed. How you decide to do it will be up to you and probably depends on your space and lifestyle. Of course, the major difference is being able to close the door of a crate if you need to keep the puppy safe. If you don't have a safe space in your house and live by a main road, it could be that a crate is a better option for you.

Whatever you decide, the first thing to say is that your puppy is not a grown dog and will have many accidents. So, as with a crate, if you do go for an open bed, I would hold off spending mega bucks on one made in Harris Tweed and Mongolian cashmere, lovingly hand-stitched by artisans at a top Parisian fashion house. Puppies don't know how to speak French any more than I do! Even poodles. And no puppy cares what shop you buy their bed from.

A dog bed needs to be three basic things:

- Comfortable

- Hygienic

- Easy to clean

A plastic tub-style bed is ideal because you can pack it with vet bedding and comfy blankets, but you can also wash it down if they have any accidents in there. The soft, pillow-like beds you see a lot of are more pleasing on the eye, but for a young dog they can seem like giant toys to be torn apart; I recommend you wait until they are past teething and better trained before you invest in one of these.

What size bed you buy depends on your dog. At one stage I lived with two Rottweilers and a Jack Russell. One of the Rotties, Gordon, took a shine to the terrier's bed and would often fall asleep at an impossible angle with his head and bum sticking out of both ends. This, despite the fact there was a perfectly adequate big-boy bed just two feet away. I loved him dearly, but Gordon was as daft as a brush, whereas you, dear reader, can make smarter choices. Just bear in mind that while you always want a dog bed to be cosy, puppies grow very quickly into their adult size and you don't want to be left with a bed they can't fit into after six weeks.

Puppy pads

Puppy pads are slightly different to vet bedding in that they are disposable, so you can use them all over the house if you want to. (They are similar to vet bedding in that people used to use something called newspaper before some clever clogs saw an opportunity to monetise puppy wee and gave us puppy pads!)

Like nappies, puppy pads are absorbent squares that you can put down around the house for the puppy to wee on. Of course, puppies don't know they are supposed to wee on them and you'll need to help them learn how (more of which, soon). But it's worth having some in for when you bring your puppy home, just to get you started on the right track. However, it's also worth remembering that puppy pads are, like disposable nappies, made with plastics and can take literally hundreds of years to decompose in landfill. If you are concerned about your puppy's carbon footprint, good old newspaper and washable, reusable vet bedding will always win the day.

Toys

As with all young animals, children included, play is such an important part of a puppy's development. Why? Because that's how they learn and grow!

Toys can help your puppy learn to track sounds, to pick things up with their paws and mouth, to carry and fetch and find. They're also a great way to build strength in their young muscles and joints, and to give purpose to all those growing gnashers. When you first bring your puppy home, it can be a good idea to have a few little toys that they can become familiar with.

The trick is not to overwhelm them with options, so just a few well-selected toys will be more than enough in these first few days and weeks. Go for toys designed for puppies with a range of textures and functions: a ball with a bell inside, something that rewards them with a treat if they work out how to get it, something to chew on, a soft toy. Quite often there will be one toy that they choose as a kind of comforter, and you might find they take that one off to the crate with them when they are tired.

There are all sorts of toys you can buy nowadays – a quick online search will reveal exactly how many. There are even soft toys with heart beats that promise to remind your puppy of their mum. As always, my advice is they don't need to be anything too fancy or overdesigned. We are not trying to create a puppy soft play area!

🐾 *REMEMBER!* Not all puppies will 'adopt' a comforter toy – don't be worried if your curious pup is more interested in your shoelaces than the little teddy bear you've given them. They're imperfectly perfect, remember!

Collars and leads

You won't be taking your puppy out for a walk for a week or two yet (see page 90 for more on first outings and socialisation), but something you can do from almost as soon as they get home is to get them used to a collar.

In the UK, the Control of Dogs Order 1992 states that any dog in a public place must wear a collar with the name and address (including postcode) of the owner engraved or written on it, or engraved on a tag. So if you are feeling extra organised, you can get that done before they come home (your local locksmith or shoe repair shop will be able to do it).

You don't have to put it on them straight away but, as with us humans when we buy a new pair of shoes or start to wear a new ring, wearing it can at first feel strange for your puppy. Having one at home ready for them means you can let them have a sniff of it and put it on for short periods of time, pretty much from day one, to help them get used to it, before the big day when they go on their first walk.

A collar will ideally fit flush to the neck but have room for a couple of fingers between the neck and the band. You can search online for average neck sizes for your breed according to age.

It's unlikely that you'll need a lead immediately, but again it can be useful to have one at home to get them used to the idea. For the early days, a simple, short puppy lead will be perfect as you want to have plenty of control. Retractable leads and longer training leads are for later on when everyone is on board with the idea of a lead.

🎾 *TIP:* If you're not sure what size lead is best, get friendly with your local pet shop owner! These guys have a lot of knowledge and want to help you find the best products for your puppy, so it's always worth asking them for guidance on sizes and so on, if you're not sure about something.

What's to Eat? Feeding Your Puppy in the First Few Days

A very special guest is coming to stay but what do you give them to eat? Knowing what to feed your puppy can be surprisingly tricky – the choice out there these days is mind-boggling. The pet food market is soaring, and increasingly it's reflecting shifts in the way we humans are eating. Vegetarian, vegan and organic dog foods, and foods with herbal remedies like chamomile and lavender to help with emotional wellbeing, are giving the old classic tinned brands a run for their money.

Whether you plan to raise a dog on a plant-based diet (arguably not what they've evolved to eat), or you're going for a traditional tripe and liver kind of menu, I think as a rule of thumb you get what you pay for. The more expensive foods cost more because they include the best ingredients. Unfortunately, it's easy to make cheap dog food and pack it out with cheap ingredients like wheat, which most dogs aren't built to digest very well. So I always recommend buying the most expensive food you can afford, at least in the first year or so. Puppies are building their adult bodies and they need proper fuel to build the best version of themselves that they can.

But no need to worry about that in the first few days. There's more on puppy diet and nutrition in Chapter 6, but for when you bring them home and everything is feeling new and unfamiliar to your puppy, think of food as the one constant you can give them. Whether you're collecting them from a breeder or a rescue centre, it's worth asking what they have been feeding your puppy on and sticking with that for a few days at least, until they are settled in at their new home. You are changing a lot in this little puppy's life overnight, so familiar food and flavours will be a source of comfort to them.

You could also have some puppy training treats in the house, as there's no reason why you can't start introducing them to the idea that these tasty treats appear when they do good things!

I used to make my own puppy treats for my Rottweilers Axel and Gordon years ago, but decided life was too short! There are some great options available now – choose something high in protein (good for muscle development) and easy to swallow without the risk of choking. You'll notice that pet food manufacturers often create food and treats for small and large breeds. If you do decide to have a go at making treats at home, there are plenty of tasty recipes to be found online. Just be sure to make the treat smaller rather than larger. You only want to give them a taste of something at this stage, not have them filling up on nibbles.

AVOID AT ALL COSTS

Chocolate! The kind of chocolate we humans consume is poisonous to dogs. It contains something called theobromine, which they can't metabolise. Dark chocolate is usually worse than milk chocolate because it has a higher theobromine content. You can still find dog treats that are made to look and smell like real chocolate – I think it's best to avoid this kind of treat as you don't want to teach your puppy that chocolate of any kind is a good thing for them.

Food and water bowls

You don't need to buy special bowls for your dog's food, although most people do like to have a designated bowl for their pups! My advice here is to go for something size appropriate that will be with you for the long haul: you don't want your Chihuahua jumping into their water bowl because it looks like a large stainless steel swimming pool. Equally, you don't want your Great Dane eating from a teacup.

Dogs can get quite excited around mealtimes, so a rubber mat to keep everything steady and protect your floor is also a good idea.

Final Word

You can have all the puppy pads and dog beds in the world but the one thing you can't buy at the pet shop is your own mental preparedness for this new arrival, coming soon to a home near you. Puppies are undeniably cute and will bring you a great amount of joy over the next few weeks and months, so be prepared to feel the love! You will be amazed at how much you can care for your new pup, how much you can miss them when they're not close by, and how responsible for them you can feel now that you are in charge.

But it can help to also be prepared for some negative feelings. You might feel overwhelmed by the chaos, you might feel disappointed by the way your puppy relates to you, you might feel anxious, tired and weary, fed up with the wee and poo everywhere. And you might feel that you regret your decision to bring this little whirlwind into your life. I can't tell you not to feel any of these things, I can only reassure you that it is quite normal to feel a range of emotions about a puppy and it's OK to have worries and concerns. The good news is that these feelings normally pass very quickly, and no matter how challenging your puppy gets, they move very quickly onto new phases of development and present you with new challenges almost every week!

Being ready to experience this spectrum of feelings can make them less of a shock and help you deal with them, if and when they come up.

Pre-puppy checklist

Use this handy list to make sure you've got everything you need in the house, ready for when the guest of honour arrives:

- Safe play area for puppy inside
- Easy to access, secure garden if possible
- Crate or bed
- Vet bedding and puppy pads
- Plenty of toys with various textures and shapes
- Puppy food consistent with their diet at the breeder's
- Training treats
- Food and water bowl with mat
- Collar with contact details
- Positive mental attitude!

So, you've chosen a name and been to the pet shop and stocked up on all your puppy essentials. And you've created a space at home where your new best friend can feel safe and secure. It can be overwhelming to think of everything, but as long as you've got these key points covered, you'll be in good shape for the big day.

Key Points

- Create an area in your home that you know is a safe space for your puppy.

- Remove all dangerous chemicals, wiring and opportunities for accidents.

- Create a cosy bed or crate which your puppy can snuggle down in.

- Be prepared for lots of wees and poos – there is no way around them!

- Make sure you've got the legal stuff covered.

- Try to think about making the transition as smooth as possible.

Next Step

Now you've got everything you need, and you're emotionally prepared for the big arrival, let's go and get them!

Chapter 3

Bringing Your Puppy Home

*It's finally happening!
Today is the day you're
bringing your puppy home*

It's a big day for you, life will never be the same again. But it's an even bigger day for the little puppy you're coming home with.

This is without doubt, the most significant thing that will ever have happened in your sweet puppy's short life; they're leaving their mum, and their brothers and sisters in the litter; all the smells and sounds and tastes that have become familiar to them will disappear in a flash, and they'll be transported to an entirely new life with you. Imagine that! It's a bit bonkers when you think about it.

Making the transition from old life to new as easy and smooth as possible will get you all off to a good start. So, what's the best way to handle this momentous occasion?

The Incredible Journey

Getting home the right way

Try to make this journey by car, not on public transport. The sights and sounds and smells of public transport will be overwhelming for a young puppy, and there's a very high chance that they will wee and poo all over you, and the passenger next to you, on the way home.

A car, ideally with a friend or partner who can either drive for you, or sit with the puppy on the way home, is ideal.

The Highway Code states that it is the driver's responsibility to make sure dogs or other animals are suitably restrained, so they cannot distract you while you are driving or injure you, or themselves, if you stop suddenly.

It may be very tempting to have your new bundle sit on your passenger's lap in the front, but really you want them to sit in the back seat so that you (or whoever is driving) can't be too easily distracted. Use a dog seat belt attachment to keep any law enforcement personnel happy. This way your puppy has contact with someone all the way home and feels secure. If you can't find a willing passenger (really? For puppy cuddling duty?) use a small crate, which keeps the puppy contained, in the boot or in the footwell in the back of the car (so that it can't fall off the seat.) Put a blanket and some newspaper in the crate and, if possible, bring a blanket square, a toy or something from the puppy's original home. This will act like a child's comfort blanket, giving them something familiar among all the new and unfamiliar sights and smells.

🎾 *TIP:* If you have to travel on your own and the crate is out of sight during the journey, keep talking or singing to the puppy on the journey home. The sound of your voice will reassure them that you are still there even if they can't see you.

🎾 *TIP:* You can also buy seat belts and booster seats for small dogs, which are a good alternative if you don't have a crate. But obviously you'll need to wee-proof the car seats with puppy pads.

How not to do it

I once met a gentleman – let's call him Dick – with a Transit van and a dog who was absolutely terrified of the van. Dick didn't understand why his dog – a little Jack Russell called Daisy – wouldn't get in the van with him. He was a builder and wanted to take Daisy along with him on his jobs.

You see a lot of tradespeople with dogs in their vans and I don't have a problem with it. The dog gets to be out and about all day instead of locked up at home, and – ideally – gets a good run or two on their travels. It's also a peace of mind thing for the tradesperson who might have valuable tools on board. They just need to be secured with a doggy seat belt or similar, as a loose pooch can cause a distraction and the fines can be pretty eye-watering for not containing them properly. And, of course, the van needs to be properly ventilated. In 2019, the RSPCA received around 8,000 phone calls in relation to dogs suffering with heat exhaustion. (That's a lot of very distressed and poorly animals, in cars that can reach temperatures of over 45°C in the heat.)

When I asked Dick to describe how he'd come to acquire Daisy, he told how he'd picked her up at eight weeks old from a breeder in Manchester and driven her all the way home to south Birmingham in the back of his empty van. This poor pup had been taken away from everything she knew and put in a giant, dark, cold and extremely noisy vehicle, and thrown around at high speed in it for two hours straight. Here was the problem then! Daisy had been traumatised by that first journey in Dick's van and had been terrified of it ever since.

Not-so-clever Dick was an extreme case. I think most of us would instinctively know that you don't leave a puppy unsecured in the back of a fast-moving Transit van for hours. But it's a useful story because as a yardstick, the further away you can get from Daisy's homecoming experience, the better. I also get to say, 'Don't be (a) Dick!' at the end of this story, which I always enjoy.

◖ *TIP:* If you do have a long journey ahead of you on the way home, give yourself plenty of time for toilet breaks (yours and the puppy's), and it's probably best not to wear your best jeans – even the briefest of cuddles at the service station is likely to result in an excited puppy tinkle.

People and Pets

MANAGING CHILDREN'S EXPECTATIONS

I always think it's worth helping children to manage their expectations about what a very young puppy is capable of. There is often a lot of misunderstanding around the kind of relationship a young puppy and a child will be able to foster, and I think we are sometimes guilty of peddling a myth about the deep bonds that children will instantly share with their puppy. Over time and with plenty of care and attention, deep bonds will of course grow. But in the very short term, most puppies will only be interested in eating whatever they can get hold of, weeing and pooing it out, and then sleeping, on whichever warm body they are nearest to at the time. They are animals pre-programmed to build a body. They're not an interactive toy. Helping children to understand this from the off can avert a lot of disappointment.

Bringing them into the house

The main thing here is to have the house nice and calm and quiet for the first time your puppy comes home. This is not the moment to be throwing that surprise 50th for your other half, with all the relatives and next door's uncle letting off a load of party poppers when they walk in.

If you've got young children at home, brief them on the importance of keeping the environment low-key and as unsurprising as possible for their new pal. This little puppy has already experienced more new sights and sounds in one day than they have in their entire, albeit short, life so gentle voices and kind hands – no tight squeezing! – are the order of the day.

Hopefully you've prepped a room as outlined in Chapter 2, and the cupboards aren't easy to get into and all the other hazards have been taken care of. So all you need to do for now, especially if it's been a long journey, is grab a brew, relax and spend some quiet time in there with your pup.

Having visitors

Just as you would with a new baby, try to keep the flow of visitors minimal for the first couple of days at least, just so your puppy can begin to get used to the idea of living in your house with their new family. It will be impossible to keep visitors at bay for long – I've never met anyone who doesn't love puppies – so you might as well resign yourself now to the fact that everyone you have ever met will be popping in and having a cuddle (with the puppy).

The upside is that this kind of coming and going into and out of your home is all good socialisation for your puppy. It teaches them that people arrive and then disappear, and they are usually friendly and bring nice things like chew toys and treats. Your puppy doesn't need to be scared of people or to protect you – their new favourite person – from other humans who come to the door.

The only thing to remember – at least until your puppy has had all of the necessary vaccinations – is to ask your visitors to wash their hands before they pick up the pup. We can all carry viruses and bacteria that don't affect humans but can affect puppies. So, until they are protected, it's a case of washing hands before and after handling.

LESSONS FROM LOCKDOWN

The UK acquired over three million new pets during the COVID-19 lockdowns of 2020, and there are some shocking statistics about the number of puppies who have since been given up by owners who were ill-prepared for the reality of owning a pup. In the UK, the Dogs Trust reported a 180 per cent increase in traffic to its 'giving up your dog' pages on its website compared to pre-pandemic visits.

As the world started to feel normal again in early 2021, one of the major problems faced by owners of these now-adolescent dogs was the separation anxiety the animals experienced. Suddenly their humans were leaving the house for hours at a time, something these dogs had never known to happen before. But there is also another phenomenon common to lockdown puppies: they never knew their owners have visitors.

I came across this problem with a chocolate Labrador I met called Bob. His owners had bought him during the lockdown, thinking, as so many did, that it would be the perfect time to get a dog. They would have plenty of time to train him and be able to take him on big, long walks every day.

They called me because Bob was having trouble walking on the lead and kept pulling them in all sorts of directions on the pavement – not an uncommon problem in youngish, jolly Labradors like him. When I turned up at their house, I walked in through the front door and Bob growled at me with quite surprising hostility. I could see Bob's owners were visibly shocked, and a little bit mortified by this. As he paced up and down the hallway, still growling at me, they apologised profusely and swore they'd never seen or heard him behave like this. In all honesty, I don't always believe people when they say that to me about their dog, but on this occasion I did. Bob's reaction was very clearly a shock to everyone in the room, not least Bob.

I sat down in the kitchen and let Bob have a sniff around and get used to me being there. Over a cup of tea, I asked them how many visitors they'd had to the house in the last year; I was wondering if Bob's hostility could be something to do with men, or people who wore cravats perhaps? It was then that they realised I was the first person who had come through the door since the start of the pandemic. Bob's new owner had a health condition that meant she was considered vulnerable, and so the only people he had ever seen inside the house were her and her partner.

Bob was simply responding to what he saw as a threat. It wasn't normal for anyone to come into his house, especially not a big man like me, and he was doing his best to protect and guard his family.

I'm not saying you should have the house full of strangers all the time, but giving your dog a healthy sense of what's considered 'normal' in your life from the start, will help you avoid difficult situations with visitors further down the line.

Introducing them to other pets

The headline news here is that the animals in your home will usually sort themselves out. There is a natural order of things, which they will find with or without you! But here's a few thoughts on introducing a new puppy to two of the most common pets in the world: dogs and cats.

DOGS

Adult dogs aren't programmed to hurt puppies. In the same way that we adults instinctively want to look after and protect children and vulnerable people, dogs don't generally have it in them to go mauling the younger members of their species. You may find your existing dog takes their new sibling under their wing immediately and you won't need to manage their relationship, but if they're looking a bit apprehensive about the new arrival, follow these rules:

- It is the adult dog and not the puppy who needs your signals most in this situation.

- Keep your adult dog on a lead at first if necessary, but give them plenty of space and time to have a sniff and get used to each other outside of the crate or bed.

- Remain calm at all times; your voice needs to let them both know that everything is OK.

- The 'good' behaviour in this situation is likely to be understated, like when your adult dog lies down calmly or allows the puppy to climb on them. Remember it's this behaviour that we need to praise. We want your adult dog to think, *I get a stroke when I lie down! This is great!*

- If or when there is behaviour that we don't want around the new puppy, like pawing at the cage or being overly excited, let your adult dog know this is not OK. You can use whatever command you like, but I like to use *ENOUGH.*

WORD UP: *ENOUGH*

We all need a word we can use when we want to let our dogs know that whatever they're doing needs to stop. And for a lot of people that word is actually *STOP.* Others prefer a straightforward *NO.* I've always used *ENOUGH.* There's something very flat and clear about the two syllables in *ENOUGH* – it leaves little room for misinterpretation. Single words like *STOP* and *NO* are strong, but with a slight upturn can easily become questioning in tone, or sound playful. *ENOUGH* seems to me to have the right vocal impact to make it very clear to a dog who might be busy doing something they shouldn't, that it's time to stop. We tend to deliver it in a non-negotiable, firm way too, whereas '*STOP!*' or '*NO!*' can all too easily sound panicked, and that's the last thing you'll want.

CATS

If your puppy is eight weeks old or thereabouts, introducing them to your cat should go smoothly enough. Your puppy's prey drive won't have kicked in yet, and as long as your cat has some space to climb up high to, they should hopefully be pleasantly curious about each other. Some cats might be more inclined than others to hiss and make a show of standing up for themselves. Try to keep their meeting positive in your puppy's mind, praise them when they're being passive or gentle, and if there is any sign that they're going to start chasing the cat, hold them back gently. Try to do this every time, so that the dog does not begin to associate the cat with chasing – even if it's just a game to them, you don't want animals firing off all over the house.

Beds, Baths and Beyond

Introducing them to their crate or bed

Puppies sleep a lot – up to 20 hours a day in some cases! How can they possibly sleep so much, you might wonder? Well, when they're asleep they're not just being lazy and having great dreams about their favourite chew toy, they are actually very busy growing and processing all the exciting things that have happened to them in the last little awake period they enjoyed. So do not worry overly about a puppy who seems to be asleep all the time. Trust that nature is working her magic, and enjoy the peace and quiet. It won't last forever, believe me.

Eventually, you want to get your puppy to the stage where they will happily snooze through the night in their crate or bed, and might even take themselves off for a nap there in the daytime. So, the sooner you introduce them to their lovely new crate or bed, the sooner they'll be able to make nice associations with it and see it as somewhere they are happy to spend time.

The first thing you need to do is position the crate somewhere that feels safe. By which I mean against a wall or under a table or somewhere that feels enclosed; speak to their natural drive to seek protection from cold and harm. Pop a couple of puppy training treats in the crate and leave the door open. (You can let them see you putting the treats in at first, but later on do try to make them magically appear inside the crate – we want our pup to think the treats grow freely in the crate.)

Next, bring them over to play near the crate and let them find their own way to the treats. While they're in there, they'll probably have a good nosey around. Make sure the door is open and let them move freely in and out of the door. No closing the door behind them and walking off – this leads to negative associations! We want only happy thoughts when it comes to the crate. (Take your time with this process, by the way. There is no rush and it's important to get it right.)

Keep bringing your puppy over to hang out by the crate and letting them go in and out of their own accord. Keep the treats appearing in there, so that they come to rely on the fact that there are always nice things for them in the crate.

Once you feel this concept has been established in your puppy's mind, you can start to close the gate occasionally, and then open it again. The idea is that your puppy sees that although you do close that gate occasionally, you always open it again. There is nothing for them to get stressed about. And meanwhile, they'll just enjoy one of these delicious treats that are always in this lovely cosy crate.

Continue doing this for longer stretches of time, until they begin to feel completely at ease with you closing the gate of the crate.

One thing to note: if they seem upset at the door being closed and begin to bark, try not to open the door while they are barking. Wait a moment until they pause. You don't want to create a problem where they think the door opens if they bark. It's better to make the association: *The door opens when I'm quiet.* The message to the puppy is 'The crate's a lovely place. Sometimes the door is open, sometimes not, but if you find you're closed in, don't panic.'

In the future, you may or may not decide to keep the crate, depending on how much space you've got. But whether you keep it or not, almost everybody has a dog bed in the house eventually. Creating a bright and happy *GO TO BED* command now will help you establish good habits around an open bed for the future. See the photo section for a photographic guide on how to do this.

Get DAPpy (wellness for dogs)

Have you heard of Dog Appeasing Pheromone? This product has been around for 20 years or so and can really help a nervous puppy settle into a new environment. Boffins somehow managed to recreate the comforting pheromones released by a nursing mother dog and bottle them up so that puppies can receive all the same comforting pheromones in their new home. They come as plug-in diffusers, sprays and wearable collars (avoid the collars until your puppy is a bit older as they carry a risk of strangulation). I would recommend having some DAP plugged in close to the crate if it's in an enclosed space, such as an alcove, or sprayed onto the blankets and bedding inside the crate. And try to keep its use mostly to the evening time, so that your puppy begins to associate that lovely snuggly feeling with the night-time.

One thing: the carrier for the active ingredient in DAP is a form of alcohol. You spray it and the alcohol flashes off in much the same way it does with a hand-sanitising gel. If the alcohol has not completely evaporated and the puppy gets a whiff of it, it can sometimes have the very opposite of the desired effect to their super-sensitive nose (think: smelling salts!). Check the instructions on your pack and make sure you leave plenty of time for the alcohol to disappear, usually around 20 minutes.

Using puppy pads in the first few days

It's worth accepting early on that the first few days at home with your puppy are going to be slightly chaotic when it comes to their toilet habits.

Some people try to circumvent this uncomfortable truth by lining their whole house with puppy pads. This is a short-term win, but a long-term loss. Yes, it will keep your floors dry, but equally if you have pads everywhere, your puppy will never learn to distinguish between where it's OK to wee and where it definitely isn't. It's also worth remembering that even if they do wee and poo on their pads, they are still doing it inside your house – and that is not what we are aiming to achieve here!

Still, they can be helpful and you might as well have a couple around from the start. I recommend putting one at one side of their crate because, like most animals, puppies instinctively don't want to wee where they sleep. So, if they are all cosy on the vet bedding at one end of the crate, they will more than likely choose to wee on the puppy pad at the other end of the crate.

Place another one by the back door, so that when they are pootling around and notice the pad by the door, they will recognise it as similar to the one where they did a wee in the crate.

Eventually, you will begin to move the pad outside of the door and your puppy will discover the joy of doing their business on the grass. Until then, puppy pads are a means to an end.

⬤ *TIP:* If you're in a flat, keep your puppy pads by the entrance door and, later, just outside in the hallway, if possible. Your puppy should get the idea that if they hang around at the door they can get to the pad outside and a human will be along very soon to take them out. Observation skills required.

Getting through the first night (and the next night)

It's been a long day, everyone is tired and it's time for bed. But what do you do with your newest member of the family?

With a few exceptions, such as night workers (been there, done that, got the bags under my eyes!), most of us go to bed at night when it's dark and wake up in the morning when it's light. And if you are anything like me, you need a good eight hours of undisturbed kip, preferably in your favourite sheets, in order to be able to face the world.

But your new puppy has spent the first eight weeks of their life cuddled up with their mum and their litter, feeding and snoozing whenever the fancy takes them. Getting them on board with the concept of a straight eight hours is probably going to require a little assistance.

There are two schools of thought when it comes to sleep training a puppy:

1. CRY IT OUT

As the name suggests, this method involves letting your puppy cry when they wake up in the night. Instead of going to them and cuddling them until they fall asleep again, you let them cry until they realise you're not coming to get them and eventually settle themselves down and nod off. As with babies, this method has its opponents, many of whom say it's cruel and can lead to anxiety in an adult dog. Supporters of this method like the fact that it works quickly – puppies usually get the idea after a night or two – and encourages the dog to find ways to settle themselves. This means that later on if, say, you need to go to work and leave your dog for significant periods of time, they are already accustomed to the idea and, hopefully, don't spend the whole time crying while you are away.

2. CAMP IT OUT

This method involves having your puppy in their crate in your bedroom at night, so that they know you are nearby and – hopefully – don't cry because you are in the same room. Over time you move the crate further away from your bedroom, maybe to the door on the second night, the landing on the third, and so on (but please don't leave a puppy somehow balanced on the stairs!). Supporters of this method agree that it is a more humane and gentle approach for the puppy. Opponents point out that there are no guarantees about how long it will take for your puppy to get the idea, and meanwhile you have a crying puppy in your bedroom and two hours to go before you need to get up and go to work.

I can't tell you what the right way to do it is – so much will depend on your lifestyle: do you have a demanding job that requires razor-sharp reactions? Your own personal attitudes: are you a black-and-white kind of person or more inclined to go with the flow? And, of course, your puppy. Some puppies love nothing more than sleeping all night and you have to wake them up in the morning. Others can't stop jumping around 24/7.

The only thing I can say with confidence is that if your puppy is properly fed and watered, and they are safe and comfortable in a secure space, it is highly unlikely that anything bad will happen to them during the night. At this stage it is important that you are well-rested and can take care of them properly, so take the time to consider your puppy's needs within the context of your entire household's.

Whatever you decide to do, you'll find that your puppy will eventually pick up on your routine.

Now, hopefully you've had a good trip home and introduced your puppy to their new family. Safety and security are paramount during these first few days, so just take a moment to make sure you've got these key points covered and enjoy getting to know your puppy.

Key Points

- Make the journey home as calm and reassuring as possible.

- Make the journey home safe and legal.

- Keep the house quiet and visitors to a minimum in the first few days.

- Think about sleep and what is going to work for you and your household.

- Keep everything positive!

Next Step

Socialising your puppy is vitally important and the best thing you can do for them to help them live a happy life. It also happens to be loads of fun, so let's get started.

Chapter 4

Socialising Your Puppy

*Giving your new puppy the confidence
to explore safely with their natural
curiosity and plenty of enthusiasm*

What Is Socialisation?

People's faces usually light up when I mention socialising puppies; they imagine I'm suggesting they go with them to the pub and take them to lots of fabulous parties.

Although both of these things can and should be encouraged as part of a wider socialisation effort, socialising your puppy is something slightly more serious and vitally important for their development, although as with all things puppy, it is never dull.

So, what does socialisation actually mean? Put simply, it's the process of getting your puppy accustomed to all the different things they're going to see, hear, taste, touch and smell as they grow up. It's about helping your puppy become confident in the ever-changing and surprising world you both live in, encountering everyday situations and people without fear, and encouraging them to generally feel like a bit of a cool customer.

In psychology, we talk about stimulus and response. So when, for example, we see a fire engine barrelling down the road at high speeds making a loud woo-woo noise, that's a *stimulus*. Our response is not to run away from it or start trying to fight it, but to accept that this extremely fast and loud red cuboid on wheels is on its way to help someone. We don't react overly in any way at all, because at some point we've programmed our brains to understand that this strange-looking thing is not a threat. For puppies, new stimuli are happening all the time. They can be anything from the sound of a bin lorry crashing about outside to the sight of a new friend with a big beard and lots of tattoos, you in a new hat or the ringtone of that man's mobile phone. What we are aiming for in socialisation is to cultivate a response to the myriad stimuli that come your puppy's way, which helps them say, *This is cool, I'm OK with this because I've already seen/heard/felt it and I know it's nothing to worry about.*

Why do we need to put a name on it, you might ask? Surely just getting out and about will teach your puppy everything they need to know? That is true to an extent but, ideally, we put a socialisation structure into their early lives in order to cross off things they might come across later on. If you live in the Scottish Highlands and rarely leave home, you may only need to socialise your dog to the sounds of rutting deer. But if you live in central Wolverhampton, rutting deer are likely to be less common. Basically, the more 'buffering' you can build into your puppy's social capabilities now, the less likely you are to find yourself in tricky situations with a dog who is freaking out about something they have never encountered before. When socialisation hasn't been sufficient, you can end up with a dog who is nervous or aggressive, or aggressively nervous, when new or slightly scary things come their way.

As a trainer, I've come across plenty of dogs who haven't been sufficiently socialised and sometimes it can make their life extremely stressful, as well as their owners' lives. You may have seen me working with dogs on television who are scared of tiled flooring or won't get into a new car. It sounds a bit silly, I know, but if you've got a dog who has only ever walked on carpets and you move to a house with only cold tiles throughout, your dog is going to think: *Hold on, what's this?* A dog who has experienced a number of different surfaces under foot will take this new experience quite literally in their stride, whereas the puppy who has only ever known carpet at home might react differently and refuse to tread on the cold tiles because they are scared of them. Ultimately, none of us wants a dog who is triggered by everyday situations. You want them to enjoy life and be comfortable.

Over on page 95 you'll find a checklist for socialisation. It covers many of the basic everyday situations you and your puppy will encounter. But there's also some space at the bottom of the checklist for you to add in some situations that are peculiar to you and your lifestyle. For example, if you're a builder and you're going to be taking your dog to work in the van with you every day, your puppy is going to need to become familiar with the sounds of a pneumatic drill or a concrete mixer, and probably Heart FM blasting out on the radio. If you work in a care home and your dog is coming in with you as a therapy dog, they're going to need to be relaxed about new people coming and going all day, deliveries and sing-a-longs.

I once met a dog whose owner was a marriage guidance counsellor who worked from home, so for them the sight of people being upset and crying was an everyday occurrence. Now, I'd be a bit worried if my dog thought that was normal, but you get the idea!

🐾 *REMEMBER!* The great thing about socialisation is that if you are doing it in the right way, you can't ever do too much.

Separation anxiety

We hear a lot about separation anxiety in dogs, especially since the lockdowns of the COVID-19 pandemic. Many dogs, especially new puppies who were brought home during the lockdowns, spent an inordinate amount of time at home in the company of their families, and rarely experienced being left alone at all, let alone for hours on end.

As the lockdowns lifted and people went back to work and school, many dogs struggled to acclimatise to these new extended periods at home without anyone else around. But it can also happen if, for example, a member of your household leaves home, you move house or start a new job that involves longer periods of time away from the house. It's one of, if not the most common problem, I am asked to help owners deal with.

So, what does separation anxiety look like? It can manifest in many forms. Some dogs become destructive and chew and scratch excessively while their owners are away, others might bark and howl. Some might pace and circle, or try to escape, and others can wee and poo – and even eat their poo – while they are in a state of high angst. However it presents itself, separation anxiety is not a pleasant thing for a dog, especially a puppy, to go through. In certain cases it can also be dangerous, especially if they escape or harm themselves while scratching furniture or chewing something inappropriate.

So how do we fix it? Well, ideally, we avoid it in the first place! It should, of course, go without saying that in a perfect world if you are considering taking on a puppy, you should be able to be at home with them, ideally for the first six months at least. Of course, we don't live in a perfect world and this book is very much about bringing up a dog who's perfect for you in an often imperfect world. I love hearing about the progressive companies who are now offering proper puppy leave to their employees. It might sound a bit gimmicky, but it really can't be taken seriously enough; young dogs need to feel looked after and form attachment bonds with their owners in the same way all young creatures do.

But even if you are lucky enough to be able to work from home, you are going to need to occasionally leave the house without your dog for a few hours, and trust that they will be content enough to not eat the sofa while you are gone.

In this sense, avoiding separation anxiety should be a key part of your puppy's socialisation programme.

Dogs are naturally social animals and being alone does not come easily to them. As such, we need to gradually get them used to the idea that being by themselves will happen occasionally, that it is okay, and that you do always come back. Try to avoid a 'cold turkey' situation where your puppy is suddenly expected to cope with you being gone for eight hours and instead, make the time to practise being apart from you.

You can do this without even leaving the house at first. Choose a time after a walk or a period of play and activity and put your puppy in their crate or a secure room such as a utility room. You may hear some pining and scratching at the door, but if you know that they are tired, it should very quickly recede as they drop off to sleep. If you think you can do it without waking the dog, open the door while they are asleep, so that they can come and find you when they wake up. If you have a light-sleeper, just wait until they wake up and let you know they are ready to come out.

However – do not open the door when they are barking or making a fuss. Wait until the quiet moment comes, which it will, and then open the door. Your puppy needs to think, *I get it, when I'm quiet they come back!*

Keep repeating this technique, leaving it a little longer each time you are gone, so that your puppy knows you do come back and becomes accustomed to longer periods of time away from you. I can't stress enough, though, that you should start with a very short period – a minute or less – and build things up slowly. Patience is a virtue (seldom found in a woman, but never in a man, according to my grandma!).

Some people suggest you can leave a puppy for an hour of every month of their life. So, a one-month-old puppy should only ever be left for one hour, two months is two hours and so on. In my experience, it's impossible to put a rigid time frame around these things and you will be the best judge of how long your puppy can cope on their own. Do bear in mind, though, that they need to go to the toilet regularly.

Another way of introducing the concept of separation to a young puppy is to close the door behind you as you walk from room to room, so that they can't follow you. This is a great way to introduce a Variable Reward Schedule to separation (more on this in the next chapter), as you don't need to do it every time you leave a room, just occasionally. Again, if they make a fuss, try to wait for the quiet moment before you open the door.

As they get older you can begin to leave the house for short periods of time. Always make sure they are safe and can't access dangerous things like bleach and electric wiring. And try to give them something interesting to do while you are away, so that they begin to associate your absence with something they like to do.

Many dogs who are very worried won't want to eat, but some food toys that challenge your puppy to 'find' the treat inside can be a great distraction.

If you have a rescue puppy who has already experienced some kind of loss or separation-related trauma, it may be that you need to address an existing separation anxiety-related behaviour. Barking before you leave and becoming distressed at your leaving cues, such as picking up keys or packing a bag, can all be signs of a dog who is anxious about you leaving.

If you think you might have an established separation-anxiety behaviour to address, my book *All Dogs Great and Small* looks at some of the ways it is possible to solve these problems in older dogs.

A WORD ON MULTIPLE DOGS

A 2021 study by animal behaviourists at the Academy for Animal Naturopathy in Dürnten, Switzerland, found that having two or more dogs at home did not reduce the effects of separation anxiety and in many cases, in fact, made it worse. That's perhaps the opposite to what you might expect, isn't it? Using video footage of hundreds of dogs in multiple-dog households, researchers realised that anxious behaviours such as barking, howling, scratching and pacing were often made worse when any dog was experiencing separation anxiety. Single dogs left by themselves were more likely to lie quietly, while those in pairs or greater numbers essentially whipped themselves up into a state of greater angst. Interestingly, male dogs were more inclined to bark and hang around by the exit door than females. This all has a ring of truth to me. I've seen many examples of this effect from the thousands of doggy households I've visited over the years. So, if you are considering bringing another dog into your family just to 'fix' your existing dog's separation issues, you might want to reconsider!

The golden window: When to start socialisation

There is a golden window of opportunity when training a puppy, known as the 'socialisation period'. In much the same way as a two-year-old toddler absorbs information so rapidly, your puppy's brain is exceptionally open to learning new things in the period between around four and twelve weeks old. At this age, their brain is literally like a sponge and can absorb and store masses of information about the world they find themselves in. The more 'good' information they can absorb at this stage, the better adjusted and happy they will be as an adult dog.

Don't lose heart though if you have a rescue puppy who has not received the best socialisation within the optimum time frame! It is not impossible to teach an older dog good habits and to 'change their mind' about things. With lots of nurture and the kind of reward-based training outlined in this book, we can tackle almost any problems your puppy might come up against.

🐾 *REMEMBER!* If you've missed the boat and your puppy is older than twelve weeks, the best time to start was then, but the second-best time is now!

If you're bringing your pup home around the ideal eight-week mark, your breeder will hopefully have begun socialising your puppy already. They will have been to the vet for their first health check and to have had their microchip implanted. They might also have met a few new people if the breeder has introduced them to potential new owners.

So, by the time they come home with you at eight weeks old, you will have already begun socialising your puppy without even realising it! They might have had a journey in a car, heard an airplane on the way, the jingle of your keys in the front door, the voices of their new family. These are all socialisation landmarks.

Socialisation and vaccinations

Your puppy should receive their vaccinations around eight to ten weeks (see Chapter 6 for more on your puppy's health). You can begin socialisation before this time, with many of the topics you need to cover, like new sounds and the postman knocking on the door, all being readily available in your home. But before you start socialising your puppy in the big wide world, and especially before they meet other dogs, it's best to make sure they are protected from infectious diseases with their vaccinations.

This means that you shouldn't take your puppy out and about before they've had their jabs and they have had a chance to kick in. Speak to your vet about exactly when this will be, according to the date they are vaccinated. You can still take them into the garden if you have one, and if you go out you can carry them so that they are still getting access to all the sights and sounds in the real world without ever touching anything.

They can also meet other fully vaccinated dogs, so if you have friends and family with dogs who are fully vaccinated, get them over and introduce them to your puppy!

TIP: One of my favourite socialisation tricks when Axel was a young pup was to sit in the car park at the supermarket with the windows down. There is a surprising amount of activity going on in a supermarket car park! From slow-moving cars and people pushing buggies to clattering trolleys and the sounds of delivery lorries reversing, it's a great one for that period before their vaccinations have been done when you don't want to put them on the ground when out and about.

Socialisation: How do you do it?

The single most important factor in the successful socialisation of your puppy is your demeanour. It has to suggest to your puppy that everything is OK with the world.

Let's take the sights, sounds and smells of a bin lorry on bin day. You've got weird sounds, people moving about quickly, wearing high-viz jackets, the smell of diesel and of course of the bins. The whole thing has huge potential for puppy sensory overload!

Now, if you are walking past the bin lorry and behaving in a way that is nervous, or that encourages your puppy's nerves, such as holding them back or seeming to protect them from the bin lorry, your pup is going to take on your stress. They're thinking: *I was slightly perturbed before, but you look terrified so now I'm terrified too!*

What your demeanour needs to say is: 'I know it looks a bit odd but trust me, it's all fine! Nothing bad is happening. All is well with the world!'

When I'm teaching socialisation, I always like to keep in mind the image of the old-school village bobby, walking down a typical high street, taking their time, brimming with confidence and quiet curiosity, greeting everyone they meet as they go. Posture is upright, there's a smile on their face. The non-verbal message they are sending: all is well with the world.

Wherever you are with your puppy and whatever the new sensations and experiences you are introducing them to, try to keep this image in mind.

SOME OTHER SOCIALISATION POINTS

- Keep your tone of voice positive, assertive and kind.

- Say 'good boy/girl' when they are being curious. Let them know that you like it when they're not being scared or nervous.

- Body language should be breezy and confident; try not to hesitate.

- Smile! If your face is right, your body language will follow.

- Never tell them off for being scared or anxious.

- Never force them into close proximity with something they're not sure of. Come back to it another time.

- If they seems scared, do your best not to use phrases like 'good boy/girl' (as in 'It's OK, good boy!'). It's surprisingly easy to fall into this trap because we naturally feel sorry for them, but we want to avoid the association that fear = 'good boy'. Don't get any nearer to the thing that is scaring them, give them time and try not to reward the fear accidentally.

- Try to think like your puppy! Too many new and exciting experiences in one day will overwhelm and exhaust them. Introduce new sights, sounds and situations to them one at a time.

- Sometimes your puppy's 'good' behaviour will be passive, by which I mean behaviour that doesn't necessarily jump out at you, such as meeting another dog calmly or remaining quiet when someone comes to the door. The key is to look out for and praise the good behaviour; ignore the bad. Remember that sometimes no response is exactly what we're after.

🐾 *REMEMBER!* If the dog has a wobble, make sure you're not wobbling. Or, at least, make sure they can't see it. No one is perfect, after all, but your puppy might think you are!

Natural Instincts

Some dogs are naturally more inquisitive or brave than others. My two Rottweilers are a good example of two dogs who needed very different approaches when it came to socialisation. Axel simply wasn't scared of anything or anyone. Whereas Gordon, despite being a big, rufty-tufty Rottweiler, was in fact a scaredy cat, and we had to take a bit more time over socialisation.

To treat or not to treat?

Treats are always good to have at the ready and a timely treat can reinforce the best, most curious moments. Maybe your dog shows a happy interest in a florist putting a forest of foliage in her van or the decorator who looks (and smells) like he's been involved in a paint factory explosion. But unlike training specific actions and behaviours (more on this in the next chapter), socialisation isn't always the kind of behaviour you need to reward with treats. The main reason for this is that you may find they are more interested in whatever they're doing than receiving treats. In which case, plenty of praise will be just as effective. We are aiming for them to know that you are happy with them when they do good things, not that a treat is always readily available.

A word on puppy classes

And the word is: go! But hold on, why am I recommending you go to puppy classes, when I've promised you everything you need to know is in this book? Socialisation, of course! Puppy classes can differ hugely in their approach, with some being Kennel Club listed and others not, and some being frankly more effective than others. But I always recommend going to puppy classes if you can, not only for the training but for the chance for your dog to socialise with other dogs, and humans of course. If they are in the evening and it's dark, they're also a great opportunity to get them used to all the sights and sounds that happen at a time when you might not normally be out and about with them. And with a bit of luck, there'll be a cup of tea and a custard cream in it for you, too. Your local pet shop, newspaper and/or social media pages will usually have details of classes operating locally to you.

Graeme's Puppy Socialisation Checklist

Use this list to get your socialisation started, and by all means add your own ideas to reflect your lifestyle.

SITUATIONS

Being picked up	☐
Being brushed	☐
Being petted	☐
Nails clipped (or pretend touch – start gently!)	☐
Teeth examined	☐
Ears examined	☐

PEOPLE/ANIMALS

Babies	☐
Children	☐
Men	☐
Women	☐
Groups of people	☐
People with hats	☐
People with glasses	☐
People with disabilities	☐
Elderly people	☐
Men with facial hair	☐
Postmen	☐
Dogs (all shapes and sizes)	☐
Cats	☐
Birds	☐
Farm animals – horses, cattle, sheep, pigs, etc.	☐

OBJECTS

Umbrellas

Trolleys/prams

Wheelchairs

Cars

Motorcycles

Buses/trucks

Bicycles

Wheelie bins/wheelbarrows

Lawn mower

Vacuum cleaner

Hair dryer

Broom/mop

PLACES

Beach

Shops

Vet surgery

Friends' places

Parks

Car parks

Enclosed spaces/crate

Schools

Streets (quiet to busy, working your way up)

SOUNDS

Thunderstorms

Bin lorries

Children playing

Babies crying

Sirens

Fireworks

Doorbells

Kettle whistling

Skateboards

Dogs barking

Planes/loud engines

Motorbikes

Pots clanging/kitchen activity

Doorbells

SURFACES

Hard flooring

Carpet

Unstable

Puddles

Slopes

Rough grass (wet and dry)

Roads

Ice and snow if weather permits (careful they don't hurt themselves slipping)

*This space is for you to add in the aspects of your
life that might affect your puppy specifically*

Socialisation should come pretty naturally as you begin
to get out and about with your new puppy. But there are
some essential moments to tick off that will help you
and your pup get the most out of life. Check you've got
these key points covered before we move on to the next
big adventure.

Key Points

- Socialisation helps your puppy enjoy life.

- You can never do too much socialisation.

- Think about the specific aspects of your lifestyle that might affect your puppy.

- Praise them when they are being curious and well-mannered.

- Your demeanour tells them everything they need to know.

Next Step

Now that your puppy is friends with the nosy neighbour and the dogs down the road, and isn't scared of your face when you've forgotten to have a shave, it's time to get training!

Chapter 5

Puppy Training!

*Time to start teaching your
new dog some old tricks!*

Now, hopefully your puppy has settled in at home and you've started to give them some early experiences with socialisation. If they are feeling comfortable in their new surroundings, it's time to start thinking about training!

When it comes to training, I always say: all work and no play makes Jack Russell a dull boy. I think that was the phrase, wasn't it?

But in all seriousness, training a puppy for me has always got to be about achieving a sense of balance. It's great to teach your puppy all the fun tricks, like giving you their paw and rolling over (one cursory glance at YouTube and you'll find endless videos teaching you how to do these and myriad other puppy party tricks). It's cute and silly and I am all for both of those things, but that stuff is meaningless without them having really learned and mastered some of the basic commands, like

SIT, DOWN and *STAY* (although *STAY* is a funny one and we'll get to that shortly). Why are these commands so important? Put simply, they are the words and signals that will keep them safe and may even one day save their life. See them as the brakes and indicators on your car – if you didn't have them, you'd very quickly find yourself in a pile-up!

In this chapter, we're going to split our puppy training up into two sections: the basics and the fun stuff. Before we start, it's worth saying that the two areas do share one very important piece of common ground. Whether you are teaching them to sit or to give you their paw, these exercises and interactions are all about building understanding and trust between you and your puppy. And once you've got that going on, you can pretty much guarantee that everything else will fall into place.

TREATS!

Puppies are programmed to build a body; that's why they are always hungry and like eating everything in sight, which is why food is a great resource when you are training a puppy – in fact, I'd say not much beats it for training purposes. So, it's a good idea to always have some puppy training treats on hand. If you don't have time to make your own, then go for something good-quality that is high in protein and remember to include it in your puppy's daily allowance. We don't want a well-behaved but overweight puppy!

The Basics: The Super Six

If you teach your dog nothing else in life, teach them these six commands. With these six core moves, you will have a dog who isn't only well-behaved at home but who you'll feel proud of when you're out and about as well. You'll be that person walking through the park with your dog who wags their tail at everyone and comes back when you call them, and everyone will say how lovely your dog is!

1. *SIT*

I once met a dog who was ten years old and never sat down. He had been rehomed by the RSPCA, rescued from a big house owned by an old lady, where something like 60 dogs (no joke) had freely roamed the grounds and the house with little or no supervision. No human being had ever taught this dog to sit and so he didn't! He either stood, moved around or, if he needed a rest, lay down.

I thought this was an interesting insight into the natural behaviour of dogs – left to their own devices they're not inclined to sit much. So why do we want them to sit if it doesn't come all that naturally to them?

Well, it's a useful way of putting the brakes on the pram sometimes, to stop it running away. Puppies are by and large exuberant creatures and whether it's for their own safety, such as at a kerbside, or simply because you need them to calm down for a moment, being able to reliably arrange for them to sit in relative stillness is a real help for any new puppy parent.

TEACHING *SIT*

1. Place a treat between your thumb and forefinger
    and hold it next to your puppy's nose so they can
    get a good whiff of it.

2. Without letting them eat the treat, slowly trace an
    arc above and behind the dog's nose. You're going
    for a kind of howling wolf position.

3. As their nose follows your fingers above their heads
    their bottom will usually hit the ground. They
    collapse into the sitting position because the treat
    (and your face) is directly above them and they don't
    want to miss out on this treat.

4. At this point you have not said *SIT* to the puppy –
    bear with me on this.

5. As soon as their bottom hits the ground, you give
    them the treat.

6. Continue to do this over and over until eventually
    you notice that your puppy is way ahead of you.
    You lift your hand with the treat, he sits down. He
    knows how this works! You have now created a hand
    signal that indicates to him that you and he are
    playing a game together, and he just doesn't know
    what it's called yet.

7. Once this behaviour is really well established, you can start to say *SIT* to your puppy when he sits down. You are now matching the newly learned hand signal and overlaying it with a new sound signal – *SIT*. You're effectively telling your puppy the name of this great game he loves. First they learn what to do by being shown, then they learn its name.

GENERALISATION IS WHAT YOU NEED

You'll probably find that you end up doing a lot of basic training in the same room at home. For most people, it's in the kitchen or the living room. There's nothing wrong with this, but dogs can tend to associate their new tricks with specific locations. In much the same way that you might always order a certain dish at your favourite restaurant, dogs can come to believe that *SIT* is something that only happens in the kitchen. We obviously want to avoid this, as we need them to be able to sit in all sorts of places! Especially when we are out and about in cafés and at the kerbside, for example.

So, once you've perfected *SIT* (or any command) in any particular location, you can start to introduce it while in other locations, inside and outside the home. The garden, if you've got one, is a good place to start practising commands outside. And remember, your location in relation to your dog is important too. At home you probably stand directly in front of your puppy to make them sit, but at the kerb you're going to be by their side.

The main thing, once you've bedded in the basics, is to keep mixing things up, so that they come to understand *SIT* is something that happens in all sorts of places. And just to make things a bit more interesting, I'd suggest you don't always do *SIT* at every kerb. Obviously, if you're at a busy roadside they need to sit until it is safe to cross. But if you are walking your dog on a quiet housing estate and there is clearly no danger, I think it's good to cross as you would normally. This results in a puppy who is more in tune with you and your instincts, than one who is so heavily programmed that they doggedly sit at every kerbside.

2. *DOWN*

Why do we need a dog to lie down when we tell them to? For me, it's a bit like putting the handbrake AND the footbrake on: it's a more reassuring kind of stop.

The importance of *DOWN* as a command hit home to me a few years ago now, when I had my two Rottweilers, Axel and Gordon. They were, as you can imagine, an imposing pair of dogs. I was walking across a field near a training centre in Sutton Coldfield, and though it wasn't somewhere I'd ever seen people running before, suddenly a man came into view, jogging in the distance. I watched him clock the dogs and slow down; he was understandably a bit apprehensive about these two beasts who were off-lead and clearly had him in their sights. I knew the dogs had never seen this kind of fast-moving human before and I needed to have them anchored to the ground immediately – not because I truly thought they would do anything, but because I wanted him to feel safe and for them to understand beyond any shadow of a doubt that they were not to move until I said so. I called out *DOWN* in my best deep voice and they instantly hit the deck. I signalled to him that it was OK for him to pass by, and he ran on. The dogs remained in position until I was sure he was well on his way. I felt enormously proud of them and really appreciated the power of *DOWN* in that moment. I dare say the runner did too!

(Of course, there is another time when *DOWN* is a vital command to have up your sleeve and that is when you want them to lie under the table in the pub.)

Before you start: one of the biggest mistakes I see when people are teaching their dog to lie down is only ever teaching it starting from a sitting position. Remember the generalisation principle mentioned earlier; teach your dog to lie down from standing AND sitting. Firstly, it helps them not to confuse or blend these two closely linked commands and secondly, you never know when you might need it – as I did with Axel and Gordon that day we met the nervous jogger.

The Super Six

1. *SIT*

I'm using a treat between my finger and thumb to trace an arc above our puppy's nose and lure him into a *SIT*. This is the finishing point. Note I'm not saying *SIT* yet.

I've introduced the *SIT* command here, but only once I'm sure he's understood the game.

2. DOWN

First things first, I'm giving our puppy a good smell of the treat. But if he wants it, he'll have to earn it!

I'm bringing my hand down to the floor here, and I keep hold of the treat until our puppy's legs are flat on the floor.

If you've got a puppy whose bum stays up in the air, use your leg as a bridge and entice them to limbo under it. Note I'm not pushing down on his back.

As an alternative to my leg, I've found a chair with a bar that's just the right height and I'm drawing him under and forward. He's a clever boy!

3. STAY / 4. RECALL

Our puppy is thinking, *All I've got to do is SIT here and he'll come back to me with that treat.*

Puppy: *Mate, you can turn your back if you like but I'm staying put until I get that treat.*

Me: 'You're not daft!'

I'll sit calmly as long as you like but if you call me, I'll be there like a shot. Yaaaay!

5. LEAD-WALKING

Baby steps.
The message is simple:
'Step with me, get a treat.'
How easy is that?

Puppy: *Get you with your
J-shaped lead!*

Me: 'I have done this before,
you know.'

6. WATCH ME

'Don't talk to the hands because the face **IS** listening.' Clever boy! (The dog, not me.)

'There's a treat in each hand, we both know that. But staring at my hands won't get you the goods.'

The job's a good'un! As he makes eye contact, I give him the treat. Once he's understood the rules of the game, I'm introducing *WATCH ME* as a command.

The Fun Stuff

ROLL OVER / PAW

ROLL OVER: Using a treat, I'm going to lure our puppy into rolling over by taking the treat around to one side and down.

No need to lure him all the way. He's got the idea from both the *ROLL OVER* command and my body language. (If I'm not careful, I'll fall over!)

PAW: I'm offering this little lad a hand. He taps my hand with his paw and I'll give him his toy. Done deal!

Bed Training

GO TO BED

When he's not looking, I leave a nice surprise (treats) in his bed.

What's not to love? Go to bed, get treats! When I know he's got the idea, I'm introducing the *GO TO BED* command.

What a happy chappy!

TEACHING *DOWN*

1. Place your treat between forefinger and thumb and let your dog have a good smell of it.

2. Bring the treat down to the ground.

3. If you're lucky, your puppy will immediately collapse all four legs onto the floor (having their bum in the air doesn't count!).

4. Only once all their legs are flat on the floor, release the treat.

TIP 1: If they seem reluctant to follow the treat to the floor, first check if the treat is special enough. Is it something they really love? Giving them a bit of kibble might not do the trick here.

TIP 2: If they still struggle with the concept, bring the treat down and draw it under the stretcher rail between the legs of a chair, or a similar piece of furniture of the right height. Place the treat just out of reach, so that they need to bring their head down low, reaching forward under the obstruction to reach it. Alternatively, you can create a bridge with your own leg that requires them to get down low to get the treat (this is easy for me as I've got long legs – short legs and a big dog may struggle with this one!).

5. Repeat this many times so that they understand that when you hold a treat, they need to lie down to be able to eat it. Always give lots of 'good boy/girl' praise when you give them the treat (and be sure to only release it when they are fully down).

6. As you keep practising, you can remove the chair leg or the knee-bend – anything you add in you will always need to take away.

7. Luring them onto the floor has now become a newly learned hand signal!

8. Once you feel certain that they have fully understood the hand signal and can reliably lie down on the floor to receive the treat, then you can add the command.

9. I use *DOWN*. You can use any word – 'cupcake' if you really want to – but whatever your word, be sure to stick to it.

TRUE STORY

I once read a question on a forum for German shepherd owners. A woman was very frustrated because her dog didn't seem to understand when she said, 'lie down'. She wrote, 'I've tried every possible command. I've even tried saying it in German and he still doesn't understand!' By all means, try talking to your Irish setter in Gaelic or your French bulldog in French, but in all my years training dogs, I've never met a dog who only thinks in the native tongue of its breed! The command word itself only means what you program it to mean by training.

TIP 1: Never push your dog's rear end down to make them lie down. Like all of us, dogs are pre-programmed to push back at something or someone who is pushing them. When training a puppy, we are always more concerned with offering the metaphorical carrot than brandishing the stick. Incentivising with praise and rewards will always beat physical manoeuvering, no matter how light.

TIP 2: Never teach two commands in the same session. Done *SIT* in the morning? Then do *DOWN* in the afternoon. Like all of us, puppies can experience information overload.

FIXED SCHEDULES AND VARIABLE SCHEDULES

Once you get good at this training malarkey, you can start to offer treats on what's called a Variable Reward Schedule (VRS). Until now, you have been building trust with your pup by giving them a treat every single time they do the right thing. This is called a Fixed Reward Schedule. It's the best way to start because the consistency establishes that *SIT*, say, produces a treat every time. Our puppy thinks, *Bingo. I get it!*

But ideally, we all want our dogs to do the right thing even when we haven't got a pocket full of treats, right? As they start to learn the ropes, you can begin to teach them that sometimes the treat happens and sometimes it doesn't. I call this the jackpot effect. You want them to get to the point where they know that sometimes the treat happens and sometimes it's only a bit of love and praise. It's a bit like the psychology of gambling. Sometimes the machine pays out, other times it doesn't.

Whether there is a treat or it's just a good stroke and a bit of love, you are telling your dog there's a standard reward for this that is always worth having, but there might just be something really special – a jackpot – about to drop. And that, my friends, is how you get a dog addicted to good behaviour.

3. *STAY*

I'm going to teach you how to get your dog to stay, without ever having to say the word. Eh? What am I on about? Let me explain.

We all need our dogs to know when they have to stay put. It is above all else, a safety measure. You might need to get the shopping out of the car, or a child, and you want your dog to remain safely in the back of the car, especially now we have electric tailgates that ping open at the touch of a button. Or maybe you're trying to cross a busy road and need to feel sure that your dog isn't going to leap into the oncoming traffic. Perhaps you're picking up a poo and don't fancy being dragged into it!

There is a tendency to train our dogs the *SIT* or *DOWN* commands kind of momentarily. We say *SIT*, the dog sits, and we reward them with a treat. But so often we forget to build in the time element of these commands. If you think about it, *SIT* or *DOWN* should really mean *SIT/DOWN and continue to do so until I say otherwise.*

I can almost hear the light bulb going on!

It went on for me at a dog training seminar in Birmingham, back in the early days of my dog training career. We trainers were all taking a break, and a woman took the opportunity to demonstrate how she got her dog to sit and stay. We all watched as her dog sat, and then as she stepped gingerly backwards, as though she'd had a bit of an accident, saying *STAY* very loudly with every step she took back. The dog was remaining in his sitting position, his whole body quivering with anticipation of the moment he knew was coming, when she would finally say *COME* and he could bolt to get that treat.

A Bavarian trainer I was next to asked me, 'Why does she say *STAY* to the dog?' I explained that she wanted the dog to remain in its place. He said he knew what she meant, but he couldn't understand why she had to keep saying *STAY*, when she had just told him to *SIT*. She hadn't told the dog to *SIT* and then get up.

'And another thing!' he wondered. 'Why did the dog have to go to her for the treat?' I explained it was just the way we had always done it. 'But the dog is being rewarded for moving!' he laughed. And suddenly I realised, he was right. The dog was getting a treat for doing the very opposite of what she really wanted it to do, which was to stay put. 'We should always take the treat to the dog when teaching them to stay,' he remarked, sagely. It's blindingly obvious when someone points it out. Why would you do anything other than reward them in situ?

To demonstrate his point, he asked me if I wanted a coffee and I said yes, please. He said, 'OK, you sit there and I'll bring you the coffee.' He didn't tell me how long it would take, or suggest I get up and chase after him, of course. I waited patiently, my mind slightly blown by what I had just realised, and when he came back he patted me on the head and said, 'Good boy!' It was the perfect illustration of what the *SIT* command should mean to your dog: it's a deal between you both. Your dog stays sitting until you come to them with the treat (or in my case, an Americano, white, no sugar. He forgot the custard creams. Then again, no one is perfect).

He was being cheeky, of course. Bavarians are, in my opinion, the Yorkshiremen of Germany. They are usually larger than life and they like their beer. And as the saying goes, you can always tell a Bavarian, but you can't tell him much.

So, when I teach you how to get your dog to *STAY*, what I'm really teaching you is how to get your dog to continue sitting, or lying down. We are aiming for a really solid and reliable *SIT* or *DOWN* that you know beyond doubt will not be broken until you come to your dog with their reward (or eventually, no reward). Think Variable Reward Schedule!

Let's begin.

Before you start: don't even try it until you've got a really good *SIT* and *DOWN*. If your dog isn't confident in these two moves, you won't be able to achieve a good *STAY*.

The challenge of teaching a puppy to remain in situ is not to be underestimated. Puppies are naturally very exuberant animals and will instinctively want to come and inspect whatever it is you are doing over there, instead of sitting over here.

Helping them understand that they need to remain seated is about two things: time (how long should I sit here for?) and distance (how far away will you go before I run after you?).

We can't work on both of them simultaneously, so let's start with time …

TEACHING *STAY*

1. With a treat between forefinger and thumb, bring your dog into a *SIT*.

2. Wait for two seconds and give them the treat. Note that you're not moving away yet.

3. If they lift their bum, don't give them the treat and calmly say *NO*. Start again.

4. Gradually build up the time between the command and releasing the treat: try five-, ten- and fifteen-second intervals.

5. Keep doing this until you are confident that your pup can wait for at least ten seconds before they get a treat.

🐾 *REMEMBER!* Your VRS! Make it two seconds occasionally to keep your dog guessing. All good things come to those who wait.

Now we can start to work on distance:

1. Bring your dog into a *SIT* and step backwards for one second, then forward for the next second. If they remain seated, give them the treat.

2. Repeat this move a few times; it might look a bit like you are doing the samba but that's OK. (The

excellence of your hip action may be lost on your perfectly imperfect puppy.)

3. Your dog is now beginning to realise that even if you move, as long as they stay put, they will still get the treat.

4. Take two steps back, then three. Build it up over time until you are taking ten paces over ten seconds. By this stage, your puppy will be thinking: *OK, I get it!*

5. Now, try it with your back turned to them. Then you can disappear behind a door or into another room. Keep building on the trust you have already established until you feel sure that your dog really believes that whatever you do or wherever you go, they will wait, because there's a treat in it for them.

Once you have mastered this in the house, and assuming their vaccinations are all done, you can start to do this exercise in the garden, then in the park or a local field. Try to make sure you practise this move in an outdoor space that is secure. If something unexpectedly distracts your puppy and they run off, you don't want it to be into a road or somewhere they can get lost.

4. *RECALL* (or, *COME* back here!)

Pretty much everything I teach in dog training has a big emphasis on calmness. Whether you want a dog to sit or lie down or stay, it's all about being calm and praising their calm behaviour. However, when it comes to recall, I always think you can be as doolally as you like! Fill your boots and go bonkers.

How so? Well, with *RECALL* what you really want is speed. You want your dog to put down whatever it is they are doing and run happily, and like the clappers, back to you. For this to happen, your engagement and your praise needs to be both excited and exciting. *RECALL* = fun time!

It is never too early to train *RECALL*. When I first met my Rottweiler Gordon, he was a tiny six-week-old puppy. When I went to visit him, his breeder would stand on one side of the large pen with treats in his hand and say 'pup pup pup!' in a high voice, which resulted in the whole litter of tiny teddy bears coming bounding towards him. It was pretty cute, I have to say. It was clever, too. Because he had already begun to train these puppies in *RECALL*. So, start this one as soon as you get home. I always think the longer you leave it, the less reliable your recall will be.

It's reassuring to remember that as a little puppy, your little bundle of joy is pre-programmed not to lose you. They will follow you everywhere. But by the time they hit adolescence (five months to a year), they will be starting to think more like a teen! They will question your authority. The first time I let my Rottweiler Axel off in a field, I called him to come, but he took one look at me and ran off into the distance. Axel 1–Dad 0. And he wasn't even close to being a doggy teenager. I knew there and then I'd have to put a LOT of effort into dog training. I never imagined where it would lead me.

TEACHING *RECALL*

Before you start: choose your word. I use the dog's name and *COME,* but other people use *BACK* or *HERE.* The word you use is up to you but, as always, once you have chosen it, stick to it.

People are sometimes surprised that I use the dog's name. They think it might have negative associations from other times you have used it and might diminish their desire to come back to you in some way. I always use a dog's name – that's how they know that you are talking to them! But it's all in the tone of voice. A high, happy voice that makes it seem exciting is the way to go. *GNASHER, COME!*

The other thing to remember here is that we are never going to tell a puppy off if they don't come back to us (why would they come back if you are only going to shout at them anyway?). Recall must be a purely positive experience.

Push the boat out with a really special treat, perhaps a piece of chicken or a bit of sausage. Something they will go mad for.

1. Stand six inches away from your puppy and let them know there is a treat in your hand.

2. As they start to come towards you, bring the treat back towards you a bit. The idea is that we are letting them know they have to make an effort for this one. We're not giving them the treat like we did in *SIT* – we're asking them to come and get it this time.

3. Keep doing this, moving away slightly more each time. You are creating a sense of urgency, and the drive to come towards you. Your puppy is thinking, *I can get that bit of food but I'll have to speed up!* Build it up over a couple of days.

4. Once you have the move down, introduce the voice command as you move away from them. Add your dog's name (let's use Gnasher here) followed by the command – *GNASHER, COME!*

5. Your dog is thinking: *It seems as though, when I'm approaching the chicken breast, I'm hearing GNASHER, COME!*

6. Once this is well established, you can start to extend the distance that you scoot backwards with the treat in your hand. Go into the hall or the living room. Play hide and seek.

7. Now you can try it in the garden. There will be plenty of interesting distractions there so if your response seems less solid, go over it again and again until it's as good outside as it is in.

8. Eventually you can start to fade out the running backwards. The aim is that you are able to stand still like a statue and your dog will still come barrelling towards you.

TRUE STORY

Back when I ran puppy training classes in the local village hall, I one day thought it would be a great idea to hide Gordon in the kitchen for twenty minutes and have him jump through the serving hatch when I shouted, 'GORDON, COME!' He, good as gold, came leaping through the hatch like a champion thoroughbred at the Grand National. I thought this was great fun, but when I looked at my class, I realised they all looked utterly terrified at the sight of a flying Rottweiler! I learned an important lesson that day: just because you can, doesn't mean you should.

WHAT ABOUT WHISTLES?

Whistles are still commonly used for *RECALL* and, in theory, I don't have a problem with them. The good thing about a whistle is that the sound carries a really long way, so if you are on a deserted beach or moor and need to get your dog's attention, whistles can be handy. Whistles are also good for delivering a consistent, emotionless sound. So, if you are feeling a bit worried about where they are and don't want that worry to come through in your voice, a whistle is a good alternative. Whistles are also cheap! This is one piece of training equipment you don't have to spend fortunes on.

However, whistles are an extra piece of kit that you will need to take with you on a walk. And if you have only trained your dog to come back with a whistle, and you lose said whistle, you can find yourself in trouble. The emotionless sound of a whistle can be a con, as well as a pro. I've always taught my students that *RECALL* is all about creating excitement and thrill; it's hard to do that with a whistle. And while whistles can be cheap as chips, your voice is always free (did I mention I'm a Yorkshireman?).

Ultimately, it's up to you but I personally prefer to be unencumbered by the extra kit.

However, if you do decide to use a whistle, choose a number of blows (e.g. peep peep) for your recall sound, and stick to it. Consistency is everything.

5. Lead-walking

Before we even talk about a lead, we should probably mention the collar. Unless you're using a slip lead (which hopefully you're not, unless you're with a working gundog. Gundogs and working terriers tend not to wear collars because they can get caught in the trees and bushes when they are out and about) you're going to need to attach your dog's lead to their collar. Now, hopefully you've been putting their collar on for short periods of time since they came home and your puppy is used to the sensation of having something around their neck.

I'm often asked if, as they get older, you should leave their collars on all day. Many people choose to take them off when they come home from a walk, believing it to be uncomfortable, or else because it flattens the coat around their neck. As with most of these things, it's a personal choice. I've always left my dogs' collars on, partly because it just seemed easier and partly because I've always lived in residential areas, where if they somehow escaped, they could be facing quite grave danger with traffic and cars. At least with a collar on, all your contact details will be there and if someone finds them, they know where your dog lives.

🎾 *TIP:* This is a great time to tap into all the knowledge at your local pet shop. The big out-of-town and online pet stores can be handy and have a wide range, but your local pet shop staff tend to really know their stuff and won't sell you something you'll be returning in five minutes. Plus, you (or rather, your dog!) can try things on in the shop until you find the right thing.

🐾 *REMEMBER!* Your dog's collar needs to show your name (not your dog's name) and your full address. A lot of people tend to only use the dog's name and a phone number, but this is not actually legal! Personally, I would also add in a mobile number if you have one, so that the person who finds them can call you sooner rather than later.

LILY
23 Puppy Lane,
Cotswolds, GL7 DOG
07000 000 000

COLLAR OR HARNESS?

The next question people often ask is whether their dog needs to wear a harness as well as, or instead of, a collar.

I wish I could tell you that the answer is one thing or another. But the truth is, it's a bit messy. If you've got a large, powerful or lively dog, such as a German shepherd or a boxer, you'll be thinking not only about leading your dog on your walks but about being able to manage their power – for example, to stop them chasing something or jumping up and down at a busy roadside. With a dog like this, and assuming they can easily breathe, a collar sat high on the neck will give you more controllability. How so? Because with a harness, a strong dog really just sees it as something to put their chest into. You're almost making the dog stronger with a harness, literally harnessing their power as you might a carthorse!

Equally, if you have a brachycephalic dog like a pug or a French bulldog, breeds which suffer with restricted airways, you don't want to attach your lead to their collar, because pulling it too hard could literally choke them.

Every dog is unique, so the decision will ultimately rest with you, and it might be that you end up trying a few different configurations before you settle on something that works. That said, I often tend to recommend a front-pull harness, where the lead attaches to a ring on the harness at the front of the chest, rather than on top at the dog's back. This style gives you all the benefits of your dog being able to easily breathe (we are never interested in choking a dog), but if you do need to guide them in a particular direction, it gives you a bit more movability or pull than a top-attaching harness.

TIP: Make sure that your harness is actually designed for the lead to attach at the front. Some come with small and insubstantial loops that – if they don't stand up to the job – can land you in hot water when the loop breaks and you are left with a lead, but no dog. Some front attachments are designed to hold an ID tag and not a lead.

FORGET CALLING IT *HEEL*

Eh? What am I talking about now? You've probably picked up by now that I like to teach a dog certain behavioural cues before we start putting a name on it or, in this case, a lead. And when it comes to lead-walking, the behaviour we are really after is having your dog walk relatively nicely alongside you.

At shows and competitions, you'll see dog owners doing *HEEL* in a way that keeps the dog's eyes on them at all times. It might look impressive in an obedience competition, but when you're out and about in town or at the park, you probably don't want a dog who only looks at your face as they are walking along! Apart from looking kind of strange, they'd miss out on all the fun smells and sights and sounds. So, we're not going for that kind of obedience here but a puppy, instead, who reliably walks by your side and ideally doesn't pull the lead, or you, all over the place. And the great thing is that you can start to teach lead-walking at home, before they've had their vaccines and before they've ever seen a lead.

Incidentally, you'll often see people with adult dogs pulling on the lead, shouting, '*HEEL*!' as they drag the dog back into line. Their timing is all wrong. The only time the dog hears *HEEL* is when they're pulling. *HEEL* ought to mean 'walk alongside me calmly', but it doesn't to these dogs. They think it means *PULL*, because that's what they are doing the only times they hear the word. Dogs are logical. Humans are weird.

LEFT OR RIGHT?

In obedience competitions, you'll see the dog is always on the left-hand side of the trainer. Why? No other reason than it makes the line look orderly when the judge is viewing them.

You can walk your dog on your left- or right-hand side, whatever side comes more naturally is fine (and if you have two or three dogs, sides tend to go out of the window!). The important thing is that you choose a side and stick to it. For the purposes of this lead-walking exercise, I'll assume your dog is on your left-hand side at all times.

A few years back, I was helping a woman train her puppy, and we were walking around her local housing estate in Northampton one evening. She had quite bad arthritis in her left hand, so we were using her right hand for holding the lead. A chap came up to us out of nowhere and said, 'Excuse me, but you're doing that wrong! A dog should walk on the left!' I nodded and asked him why that was. Slightly taken aback, he said he didn't know but that they should just be on the left. Proper trainers always do it that way. Luckily, I was able to explain to him that the landed gentry, since time immemorial, had walked around their estates with a gun in their right hand, and that was where the tradition of having a dog in the left hand, away from the gun, came from. 'And as far as I know, this lady isn't in the habit of walking around Kingsthorpe with a shotgun.' He thanked me for clearing that up and we said our goodbyes shortly afterwards.

TEACHING WALK

1. Get your dog to *SIT* on your left-hand side. If they haven't learned *SIT* yet, you can just try to get yourself on the right-hand side of them. (This may be tricky depending on how excitable your puppy is!)

2. Let them know you have a treat in the hand closest to them (your left hand) by dangling it in front of their nose.

3. Step forward and lure them forward with the treat at the same time.

4. If they move forward with you, give them the treat.

5. Don't release the treat until they have moved in time with you.

6. Keep doing this move and adding in another step forwards.

7. Walking slowly, keep them in position and only give the treat when they maintain the right position.

8. Your puppy is beginning to realise that the key to opening the hand with the treat in is to follow you and stay in this position!

9. Now your puppy can walk alongside you, we need to link you together with the lead.

SHALL I LEAD?

In the olden days of dog training, when people used choke collars and other unpleasant ways to get their dogs to behave, the 'correct' way to hold a lead was with two hands across your body and the dog to the left at your feet. The thinking was that two hands on the lead made you stronger. Thankfully, those days are long gone and we no longer use leads to manhandle our dogs. Leads are a safety precaution, to be activated when your dog sees a squirrel or runs into the road. I always say that if you have trained your puppy the right way, no one should need two hands and all their bodily strength to walk their dog on a lead.

For me, the ideal way to hold your dog's lead is in what I call a J-shape hold. Hold your lead with your left hand, with your thumb facing forward, your arm dangling freely and the lead at such a length that it forms the curve of a letter J as it falls. If you do need to pull the dog, you're in a natural position to do so.

Why J-shaped? Why not really short and close to you, or longer and looser so that they can be freer? Put simply, if the lead is too short the dog will pull you. It's called an 'opposition reaction'. It is nothing to do with politics, but the simple fact is that like all of us, a dog will react to being restricted. Short lead = pulling dog. You pull one way, the dog pulls the other. Similarly, if it's too long the dog will get too far in front and trip you up. (And, as a lead is a piece of safety equipment, that seems like a silly outcome!) A good J-shaped lead will help you avoid too much slack.

🎾 *TIP:* If you've had dogs before, and particularly ones that pulled, your muscle memory could be your worst enemy. People who are used to feeling tension on a lead often subconsciously pull back until they feel some weight at the end of the lead, triggering an opposite reaction from the dog. That's what feels normal to them and, funnily enough, every dog they ever owned pulled. You might want to watch out for that particular shot in the foot.

TEACHING LEAD-WALKING

Now it's time to get them to walk alongside you, but with the lead connected to the collar. Here we go:

1. Have a treat ready in your left hand, or the one closest to the puppy. (Using the opposite hand can encourage them to go across you and we want to avoid that.)

2. With your puppy on a J-shaped lead, step forward as before and give them a treat if they step forward with you.

3. Next, extend the distance and take a few more steps before you give them the treat.

4. Remember your VRS! Give them a treat at random distances, to keep them guessing.

5. Now we've got a dog who is walking alongside you on a lead!

Once you have cemented this exercise with plenty of practice, you can start to throw in some corners and bends.

TIP: Your ideal position is with your puppy's shoulders alongside your legs. Why? Because any further back and you'll lose sight of your dog. Any further forward and they can't see you!

WALKING MANOEUVRES

Turning left
For this, I'm assuming your puppy is on your left. Reverse these instructions if they're on your right. This is usually easier because your lower legs come towards the dog as you turn, they see you easily, and your body gently guides them: they will see the leg coming and move themselves out of its way. This is not about kicking or pushing them with your leg, rather gently guiding them with the physical motion. As soon as they make the turn, give them a 'good boy/girl!' They begin to understand that they you're happy when they walk in a straight line AND when they turn left.

Turning right
This is trickier as it involves physically turning away from the dog. Your puppy doesn't see your leg coming towards them or looming large in their field of vision. It's a bit like a car disappearing in your rear-view mirror; when your leg is going away your dog's brain doesn't necessarily register it. It may be that your puppy twigs it and comes with you of their own volition; if this happens, praise that moment. Reward all good decisions!

If they don't, use the lead to gently nudge them and remind them to come with you. This shouldn't be a drag or a pull that means their opposition reaction kicks in. It's just a nudge to remind them you're going this way. Use a high voice and warm tone to say their name if necessary. It's never forceful, just a nudge in the right direction.

SLOWING DOWN AND SPEEDING UP

Mix up your lead-walking even more by walking slowly and quickly. Don't say anything to your puppy – they need to be able to react to your physical cues here. To slow down, take baby steps (rather than walking in slow motion) and only reward your puppy when they get to the optimum position, with their shoulders at your legs. Next, you can try to speed it up. (You're not trying to trick your dog here, so don't burst into your best Usain Bolt setting a world record!) Just speed up a bit and give them a treat when they adjust their speed and, as always, have their shoulders level with your legs.

GOING OUT FOR FIRST WALKS

Once your puppy is used to walking on the lead in the house, or the garden if you have one, and assuming their vaccinations are now active, you can start to take your puppy out for walks to the park or any other open spaces near to you. This is a super-exciting time for them as all the smells and sights and sounds of the outside world start to come into view, literally and metaphorically.

Now, one of the great things about walking the dog, and one of the big reasons people decide to become dog owners in the first place, is that it's an easy way to build exercise into your daily life. It's also something that you can combine with other activities, such as walking the children to school or meeting up with friends.

I'm all for mixing up your dog walks with friends and I know only too well how busy life can get; if you can combine a dog walk with an important phone call or an errand you need to run, what's not to love about being able to do that, eh? However! If at all possible, your first walks out in the real world with your puppy should be entirely focused on them and everything that is happening during their walk.

As is the case in almost all of the training we are talking about in this book, it is vitally important that you are able to notice and praise good behaviour as and when it happens. This sends a clear message to your puppy that you like what they are doing, and they in turn understand that whatever they are doing when you notice and praise it, can and should be repeated.

If you are walking your puppy but also nattering away with your headphones on, or trying to listen to a child, it's likely you'll miss opportunities to reinforce good behaviour when it happens. So, if possible, schedule in some time to really focus on your puppy's first proper walks out in the big wide world. You will reap the benefits for many years to come!

FIRST PROPER WALKS

It is inevitable that your puppy will be excited and want to smell all the interesting things on your first walks out in the world. We don't want to dampen that natural curiosity or have them lose confidence in their inquisitive nature.

After all, we've taught them through the socialisation training that we approve of these characteristics!

Equally, you need to maintain a safe and steady position as you walk along the pavement or in the lane and ensure that you can't be pulled all over the place as they lurch from one new smell to the next, if you want to be able to walk them alongside a buggy, for example.

So, just as we did at home when they were first learning to walk alongside you, allow them to explore and look at things, extending the lead slightly to give them that extra bit of manoeuverability. But try to maintain the J-shape (a good marker is not allowing the lead to drag on the floor) and only reward them with treats and praise as and when they come back into that 'sweet spot' position, with their shoulders parallel to your legs.

Keep the treats in your left hand (or the hand closest to your puppy) and if your puppy jumps up or walks across you, quietly and gently stop. Wait for them to come back into the correct position and then reward them with a treat and/or praise and continue your journey. They will begin to realise that they can have a good nose around (and do let them have a good sniff when it suits you), but still need to stay close to you as you travel to your destination.

EYE, EYE!

Dogs have incredible peripheral vision, far better than us humans. When they're looking straight ahead, your puppy can actually see 240 degrees in front and behind, compared to the 180 degrees that humans can. That's pretty much two-thirds of the 360 degrees in a circle. Some dogs also have a high-density line of vision cells across the retina, called a visual streak, which lets them see a sharply focused object in the distance, even in the far extremes of their peripheral vision. They can literally see out of the corners of their eyes! Some dogs, like sighthounds, are even more attuned to movement and with slender heads get an even better view in their rear-view mirrors.

dog's field of vision

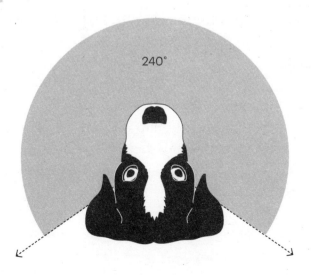

240°

6. *WATCH ME*

Why do we need to teach eye contact? You might think that your dog already gives you the puppy-dog eyes quite a lot, so why do you need an extra command? Well, there will be times when you urgently need your dog's attention. It might be very important that your puppy listens to you at the side of a road, or understands it is time to leave somewhere and needs to get their lead on. Eye contact is a command that tells your dog to watch you and await further instructions.

As ever, actions speak louder than words. We're going to teach the action first and add the command once we're sure your pup knows what they are meant to do in this game. This one is simple and really good fun! It's all about making a positive association with looking at you.

TEACHING *WATCH ME*

1. Start with your dog sitting in front of you. Hold your hands out to each side and have a treat hidden in each hand.

2. Let your puppy work this one out by trial and error. It's a puppy puzzle. Any puppy worth their salt will keep sniffing both hands, but what we want them to learn is to stop looking at the hands and look you straight in the eye.

3. When the above happens, give them a treat.

4. Our puppy is thinking, *When I look away from the treat and directly at my owner, I create an open sesame moment!*

5. Reinforce this concept by rewarding them randomly from both sides. The puppy stays central and realises there is no point scanning left and right like a tennis umpire. Very quickly, they learn to look straight ahead to get a treat. They're thinking, *All I have to do is look at you! It's the easiest day's work I'll ever do!*

6. All that remains is to name the game. The message is 'Look into my eyes – not around the eyes but into my eyes.'

7. Add the command *WATCH ME*.

8. Try it when they are distracted. If you have done it right, they will lift their head up and look at you.

9. You have taught your puppy to pay attention to you.

PERFECTLY IMPERFECT PUPPY

The Fun Stuff

There are a number of what I call non-essential moves and tricks that many dog owners like to train their dogs to do. The purist (or is it the Yorkshireman?) in me thinks these moves can be a little bit too humanised. By which I mean they don't really have any useful purpose, but they look kind of cute and please people more than dogs when your dog does them right. However, the dog lover in me thinks these moves are a lot of fun and they can be a great way to help build rapport and communication between you and your pup: the all-important bond.

ROLL OVER

Rolling over is a fabulously silly trick you can teach your puppy, and with a bit of luck it might wear them out for five minutes, too.

TEACHING *ROLL OVER*

To teach your dog to roll over, first bring them into the *DOWN* position:

1. Kneel in front of them with a treat in front of their nose, close enough that your dog is really feeling like this treat is going to happen at any moment.

2. Then simply trace an arc from one side of their head, over and above your puppy's head, so that their nose follows the treat.

138

3. Do this very slowly at first. Hopefully, somewhere in the middle, your puppy will realise they need to roll onto their back in order to follow the treat.

4. When this happens, give them the treat.

5. Now you have created a hand signal with the tracing of the arc, which tells your puppy to roll over.

6. Once you have practised this a few times, you can add a name and the command: '*GNASHER! ROLL OVER.*' Hilarious.

TIP: If you want to get a bit fancy, you can teach them the opposite direction. Simply trace your hand in the arc going the other way. You can also speed up and slow down.

PAW

It always makes me chuckle a bit when people proudly show me that they've taught their dog to give them their paw. Why? Well, there's a reason why most dogs do *PAW* so readily – when dogs are anticipating something, they lift their paw. If you think of the classic pose of a gundog such as a pointer, working in the field, they tend to lift their paw as they are considering what move to make next. So, most dogs will lift a paw, but they do it even more happily if they know there is a treat in it for them.

TEACHING *PAW*

Teaching *PAW* is simple:

1. From *SIT*, kneel in front of your dog with the treat in your hand.

2. Move your hand that is not holding the treat towards the paw you want them to give you and gently pick it up. You may find it comes to you easily, or it may take a few tries.

3. When the dog's paw lifts from the floor and pats your hand, give them the treat.

4. Do this a few times until the dog understands that your hand moving towards their paw is a hand signal for them to lift their paw.

5. Only once you are sure they understand your signal do you add in, 'Good boy/girl. *PAW*.'

6. Ta-da! We have taught them a hand signal and we have given it a name.

WHICH PAW?

Can dogs be left- and right-pawed? Absolutely! Most dogs will favour one paw or another to lift. But once you have got it with one paw, you can then move on to training them how to lift the other one.

To get them to offer you the other paw, you simply give them the same hand signal but on the other side. You can say *PAW* again, and gently tap their lower leg as a nudge.

There is one dog breed you might not want to overdo *PAW* with: boxers. They got their name for a reason. Big, lovable clowns, they will happily bat away at you with their paws for attention given the slightest encouragement. Personally, I love it, but many people don't. You might choose not to encourage *PAW* in boxers and other big breeds, with paws that might be harmful to children or the elderly.

SPIN

If you're a fan of *Strictly Come Dancing*, you'll enjoy this move! This is similar to roll over – you're just asking them to perform it on a different plain.

TEACHING *SPIN*

1. Starting from a *SIT* position, with the treat in your fingertips, simply lure your puppy's nose around in a clockwise circle.

2. If they don't spin all the way around immediately, you can reward them at 90 and 180 degrees until they get the idea.

3. Once they know what's happening, you can get them to spin around the other way simply by reversing your hand signal.

4. Once this move is perfected, you can add in the voice signal as with the previous commands: *SPIN!* (Note, we only ever add the verbal commands at the end of each process.)

And if you do really, really love *Strictly Come Dancing*, you could name this move after your favourite dancer or move. There's no rule to say you have to call this *SPIN* at all, it could be *ANTON!* or even *SAMBA!*

TRAINING WITH CLICKERS

Once you get out and about with your dog, you're likely to come across people who use clickers to manage their dog's behaviour. And you might think to yourself that their dog looks very well-behaved indeed and wonder if perhaps you should be using a clicker too?

My take on clickers is that, a bit like whistles, they can be useful when used properly, and I'll explain why in a moment. But, also like whistles, people often don't use them properly and go around clicking their clickers at their dogs in the hope that it will create some kind of instant obedience response.

I'm sorry to announce that clickers won't magically compel your puppy to stop chasing after that squirrel and turn around and come back to you. In fact, they won't do anything much except make a unique sound, which you can use to tell your dog when they are doing something good. They are for positive reinforcement and are especially useful for doing this when your dog is some distance away from you, and you want to tell them you're pleased with something they have done.

So how did we come to use clickers in dog training? The roots of this method of communication with other mammals can be traced back to dolphin and marine mammal methods, and was brought to the wider world by one particular American author, Karen Pryor. Pryor realised that the principle is the same in marine animals as it is with dogs: animals repeat behaviour that is rewarding to them. The sound of the clicker marks the very moment the animal does something that you like, and it guarantees them a reward. Crucially, it allows the reward to be separate from the act.

So, how and when do you use a clicker?

Firstly, you need to get your dog used to the concept of a clicker. This is a fairly simple process. You just click the clicker and give them a treat! Repeat this a few times, until you can confidently say your dog knows that when a click happens, a treat follows soon after.

Next, click the clicker while your dog is busy doing something else that you would like to reward. Lying down is always a good one to do this with. If your dog is lying down, give them a click and hopefully they will look up and come and get the treat that they know always follows this funny sound you keep making.

I used this method with my Rottweiler Gordon, who found the *DOWN* command difficult. He didn't have the time to put his bum on the floor! He was easily bored. So instead of teaching him how to do it, I could only reward him when he did it voluntarily. So each time he lay down, I would click and then give him a treat. Before I knew it, he was throwing himself on the floor at every possible opportunity and I was running out of treats. 'You like this, Dad? Look, I'm doing it again!'

This is the difference with clicker training: you're not necessarily luring them into doing something with treats, but instead rewarding them when they do the behaviour you are looking for. Of course, it also requires you to be watching them every second of the day if you do it Gordon-style, and sometimes that's not possible. Unless you are a professional trainer, this kind of positive reinforcement makes a good addition to your toolkit, but is a hard one to live by 24/7.

So if it's so good, how come I don't use a clicker? Well I do, kind of. But instead of using a clicker, I use my voice and a marker word – a quick, sharp *GOOD!* in a high-pitched tone that I borrowed from a Scottish dog trainer I met years ago. (To this day it sounds slightly Scottish when I do it: *GUID!* The sound is very precise and I don't use it in everyday speech, importantly.) It's the clicker method, without the clicker.

This means I don't have to remember a clicker every time I leave the house, and my hands are free for all the other things I need them for. Using a marker word like this is a lot more natural to most people, I've found. If that helps you get your timing spot-on, then great!

Here's my top tip: try getting your puppy used to single-syllable 'marker' words like *GOOD* or *YES* while using treats as described above. Then start to introduce it, and the treat, when you notice them doing something you want to encourage. They'll soon realise that the behaviour you like also gets them a tasty reward!

Toilet Training

The first thing to say about toilet training your puppy is that it takes time! It's not unusual for a puppy to be four or five months old before they've completely got it, so if you're still clearing up wees and poos at 12 weeks old, and think it should all be sorted by now, please don't panic. In my experience, it is only those with unusually early toilet training success who like to boast about it – and so that's all you'll ever hear about. For the rest of us, the silent majority, it's a slow and steady process.

The second thing to say is that dogs do naturally prefer not to urinate and defecate in their own nests (aka your home), so there is plenty of innate drive to work with when it comes to toilet training. Mother Nature is on your side, so there's no need to approach this aspect of your dog's training with dread.

So – how do we do it?

As I mentioned in Chapter 2, puppy pads are, in my opinion, a bit of a red herring. It's useful to have them around the place during the very early days after your puppy has arrived home with you, simply because puppies do lots of wees and poos – especially wees – and it is much easier to clean up a puppy pad than scrub the cream-coloured carpet for hours.

So, by all means, do have them around, but it is best to avoid attempting to train your puppy to go on a puppy pad. Put simply: we want them to go outside, not inside (even if it's on a pad!).

As with all my training methods, when it comes to toilet training, the emphasis should always be on positive reinforcement. We should never scold a puppy for doing what comes naturally to them. Old ideas, like rubbing their noses in their poo or shouting at them long after the event, will only serve to create anxiety and fear in your puppy, and that is not helpful or kind.

A word on the weather: people often assume that summer is the best time to embark on toilet training a puppy. The back door will be open and your pup can come in and out freely. This is true to some degree, but as with all training, toilet training requires your attention. With the door open and your puppy moving in and out of the house, it is easy to miss the opportunities to praise them when they go to the toilet outside. It can also mean that they do not learn to make a significant distinction between inside and out, which means they may begin to seek out private places inside your house that they believe are suitable places for a poo, but you do not!

In effect, with open doors it's easy to end up with a puppy who's thinking, *I go outside and that's OK. I go inside and that seems fine too,* and with no input from you, that's not so surprising, is it? So in this sense, it really doesn't matter whether it is summer or winter when you get your puppy. There is only an ideal place to do the training: outside.

Let's begin.

Puppies are not capable of holding in their ones and twos for very long. So, we need to give them plenty of opportunities to get it right while remaining calm and not reacting if there are any accidents.

Take your puppy outside as close as you can to every 90 minutes. This will ideally include the most likely moments for them to go, such as:

- When they wake up.

- Shortly after a meal and/or a drink, when their system needs to make room.

- After playing a game or exercise (like when they are not distracted by all the fun and realise that they need a wee).

When you go outside, try to be a bit boring. By which I mean, don't engage in games of fetch or try your latest training moves. Anything too interesting will distract them. Back in the day, when smoking was more common, I used to suggest owners have a cigarette while they took their dogs outside. I'm not recommending anyone takes up smoking in order to train their puppy, but the principle is the same. Smokers tend to stand around doing little else other than smoking, and that is what we are aiming for you to be like here.

Stay outside until your puppy does a wee or a poo. It can sometimes feel like that moment will never come, usually when it is below 0°C or throwing it down with rain. But it will come! Believe me.

As soon as you see them do something, praise them with 'good boy/girl'.

🎾 *TIP:* This must be a calm vocal! We are not trying to distract them from the task in hand. A soothing, calm appreciation of what they are doing is what we are aiming for. Too excited, and they may break off what they're doing to run to you.

Your puppy is thinking, *It seems like they love it when I do a wee out here!*

Keep doing this every 90 minutes, or as close as you can get to that, and praising them every time they do a wee or poo outside. You can, if you wish, add in a voice signal such as *GO TOILET*, which can help you further down the line if, for example, you are on a long journey and want your dog to do a wee in a specific place, such as a layby.

Because they know good things happen when they do it outside, your puppy will eventually begin to let you know that they need to go to the toilet, usually by standing near the back door.

If you live in a flat, unlike a house, you can't just open the back door when it looks like your dog needs a wee. You have to open the door and maybe go down a few flights of stairs first! But in many ways, I think flat dwellers are at an advantage. Why? Because they physically need to go outside and wait with their puppy before they can go back in, and they are more likely to be paying attention when their puppy goes to the toilet.

When it goes wrong

If a puppy does start to do a wee on the floor in front of you, it is OK to let them know that this is not acceptable. Calmly and firmly say *NO* and pick them up. (Note that this is delivered in a 'nope/doh, wrong place' kind of tone, never angrily. We're teaching them, not scolding them.) They will usually stop weeing. Take them outside and if they have some left, praise them for continuing to do it outside.

If you miss the moment, there really is no point crying over spilt wee or poo! (But do make a mental note to try to spot the next one.)

🐾 *REMEMBER!* You never want to make the dog scared of you. Even if your puppy has weed on your best Persian rug, try to take the emotion out of any admonishment. If they have had an accident and you weren't there, all you can do is clean it up. You missed the opportunity to firmly but calmly tell your dog that this behaviour isn't right.

So, you and your pup are now getting on like a house on fire, you're a dab hand at everything from *SIT* to lead-walking, while ensuring that you're keeping up with the other training exercises (the fun ones too!). But if you take anything from this chapter, make sure it's these key points.

Key Points

- The Super Six (see page 104) will see you right.

- Non-essential training commands are fun to do and are good for bonding.

- Always the carrot, never the stick.

- Clickers and whistles are OK but not strictly necessary.

- Never reprimand a dog for something in the past.

Next Step

They've mastered *SIT* and *STAY* but now let's put it into practice at the groomer's and vet's as we move on to learning more about your puppy's health and haircare needs (plus a bit more) in the next chapter.

Chapter 6

Your Puppy's Health and Grooming

*Keeping your pup looking and feeling
fit as a butcher's dog*

On a very simplistic level, puppies are no different to any other animals, humans included, in that they need the fundamentals of a good diet, plenty of exercise and plenty of rest to stay in top shape. If you are looking after them on these three fronts, preferably with lashings of love and affection to boot, then you should be able to expect to be raising a healthy, happy dog.

However, like all young animals, puppies are susceptible to certain illnesses, injuries and problems. Your vet will be the best source of information about your dog's breed and their specific needs. Lots of vet clinics hold puppy parties, which, as well as sounding rather cute, are also where new owners can come to chat to the vet staff and find out more about how to look after their new puppy – it's always worth heading to one of these if you can get there, as it's also a good opportunity to form some positive associations with the veterinary clinic. If they only ever go to the vet for things that hurt, you can end up with a dog who is reluctant to walk through the doors!

So, bottom line is talk to your vet to make sure you've ticked all the boxes with your puppy's health. In the meantime, please find a few key things to consider over the next few pages.

Health

Vaccinations

Like all dogs in the UK, your puppy should receive their core vaccines, which protect them from diseases such as:

- Parvovirus

- Distemper

- Infectious hepatitis

- Leptospirosis

Your vet may also advise you vaccinate against kennel cough and rabies, depending on where you live and how much foreign travel your dog will be doing.

Vaccinations are given in a primary course, when your puppy is around eight to ten weeks old, and they should be protected a few weeks after the final injection of their primary course. You must keep them away from other dogs and potential infection risks during this time.

Talk to your vet about when it will be safe to take them out but, until then, ideally try to keep them at home unless you carry them in your arms or in a suitable bag or even a trolley.

They should then have yearly booster injections to keep their immunity at the optimum levels. Again, your vet should be able to tell you when these vaccinations are due.

🐾 *REMEMBER!* If you stop vaccinating your dog they will become susceptible to these infectious and sometimes fatal diseases, so it's important you stay on top of their boosters.

Diet and nutrition

When you first bring your puppy home it's a good idea to help the transition go smoothly by maintaining whatever diet they have been on until now. Talk to your breeder or the rescue centre about this and, with a bit of luck, they may even send you home with some of the food your pup has been eating.

Puppies grow at an astonishing rate and at times in their first six months of life, can need the equivalent of three times more calories, proteins, vitamins and minerals as adult dogs of the same breed. So, their diet is extremely important! The old adage, you are what you eat, is as true for puppies as it is for us humans.

When it comes to feeding our pets, there is now so much choice available that it can be difficult to know where to start. Many dog food options are reflecting our human leanings towards more organic, vegetarian and plant-based diets. As we all become more environmentally conscious, the impact of the meat industry and our pets' carbon footprint on climate change is becoming an important factor in the choices we make around our puppies' diets. And it's worth noting that it is technically possible to raise a vegetarian, and even a vegan, dog. Unlike cats, who are what's known as obligate carnivores, dogs have amylase genes, which means they can digest plant starch. This is thought to be an adaptation that may have developed as they ate the scraps of eggs, berries and grass that was left for them around prehistoric campfires.

However, in the UK, under the Animal Welfare Act, you have an obligation to feed your animal an appropriate diet, even if that is in contradiction to your own belief system. And vets tend to agree that, especially in young dogs, it is a safer option to go for a 'complete' puppy food that ensures all the key nutrients are in place. Most include protein (mostly animal), carbohydrates, fat, vitamins, minerals and water. A complete puppy food will contain all of these, except for water, which should always be readily available at home. Without the correct balance of these key nutrients, puppies can develop deficiencies, which can in turn cause a number of health problems, from skin abnormalities and poor bone health to sight and weight issues.

Certain breeds can also be susceptible to inflammation and allergies. Your vet will always be the best source of advice on what to feed your dog, and your local pet shop will also have plenty of great advice. Always follow instructions on how much to feed them according to their weight. And as I said earlier in the book, aim for the best you can afford, especially in the first year of their life. It's an investment in their future good health – always the top priority – but it might also save you a pretty penny on vets' bills. Buy cheap, pay twice …?

Teeth

Just like us humans, dogs are born with baby – or should that be puppy – teeth that fall out and are replaced by their permanent teeth. It will depend on when your puppy comes to live with you but if it's around the eight-week mark, your pup will still have their baby teeth – all 28 of them!

It's a good idea to have plenty of chew toys around, as your puppy's drive to chew things will be very strong. Go for a range of different textures and shapes so that your puppy can really exercise their jaw and enjoy using their new gnashers without ruining all your shoes.

TIP: Try to get your puppy accustomed to the idea of you looking at their teeth and handling their mouth from an early age. You can very gently lift their lips on each side of their mouth while stroking them and making lots of reassuring sounds. Keep doing this little and often, until your puppy is comfortable with you gently opening their jaw. This will make it easier for vet examinations and brushing their teeth later on.

At around 12 weeks, you'll begin to come across little white teeth dotted around the house, as your puppy's milk teeth begin to drop out and their permanent teeth grow in (or 'erupt' as the doggy dentists say). By six months, they should be in possession of a full set of pearly whites – 42 to be precise.

It's important to look after your young dog's teeth. Periodontal disease can be extremely painful for dogs and can lead to serious medical problems, and expensive vet bills, so it's always worth staying on top of your puppy's dental hygiene. (Brachycephalic dogs with short faces, such as some pugs and bulldogs, can have misaligned jaws and suffer with overcrowding and missing teeth, so it's especially important that you look after their teeth if you have a breed that suffers in this way.)

The best way to keep your puppy's teeth nice and clean is, of course, to brush them. Your vet can show you how best to approach brushing, so be sure to ask for a quick demonstration when you are there.

You'll need to buy dog toothpaste – never use human toothpaste – and ideally a dog toothbrush that slips over your fingers. Hopefully your dog will accept brushing, especially if you have been getting them used to your fingers being near their mouth from a young age. Most dogs come to enjoy having their teeth brushed, but if you find yourself with one who resists, dental sticks and chews can be a good replacement.

Obviously, diet is a key factor in maintaining strong teeth. Dogs don't know how to floss, so bits of food can and do stay lodged in their teeth. It makes sense to choose foods with as few additives and preservatives as possible. Dry food can also give them an opportunity to crunch and chew, which can have a descaling effect, so try to include some in their daily diet.

Neutering

Should you have your dog neutered? It's obviously a personal choice, and there is no shortage of opinion on both sides of the argument. Many people believe that neutering – which involves surgery and general anaesthetic – is an unnecessary process to put your dog through, unless there is a specific problem that it will help. Animal charities such as the RSPCA tend to support neutering, because of the burgeoning overpopulation of puppies and dogs in their re-homing and rescue centres.

Obviously, if you are intending to breed then it's usually best not to get them neutered! But you'll find that many vets recommend your puppy be neutered and there are a number of compelling health reasons why that is. But first, let's look at the basics.

In neutering-speak: young females are 'spayed', which means they have both their womb and their ovaries removed; male dogs are neutered or 'sterilised', which means their testicles are removed.

Vets often recommend neutering is done when puberty begins; for bitches that can be between four and nine months, and for males it's a bit later, between seven and ten months, but typically later for larger males. The operation is done under a general anaesthetic and is usually quite quick – you can take your puppy home shortly afterwards and they will typically make a speedy recovery.

Many people believe that neutering can cause your dog to gain weight. In my experience there's no reason why that should be so. The main cause of weight gain is, and always has been, over-feeding and under-exercising. If you are doing all the right things on these two fronts, you shouldn't find yourself with an overweight dog.

But there is a thing known as spay coat, which affects some gundogs, such as setters, retrievers and spaniels. Dogs with spay coat develop a woolier and more matte-looking coat than those who haven't been spayed and even though it affects both male and female dogs, it is still called spay coat. (Confusing, I know!) If you think you might want to show your dog in the future, or if the glossy coat of your Irish setter is not something you are prepared to sacrifice, then you'll need to think about whether neutering is the right step. Your vet will discuss this with you and help you weigh up the pros and cons of neutering. My bottom line with neutering is to consider it on a case-by-case basis. I've had both neutered and un-neutered males and a spayed female in the last few years. That aside, some of the health benefits of neutering include:

- In male dogs it can reduce the tendency to mark their territory with urine (aka cocking a leg).

- In female dogs, it stops any bleeding associated with being 'in season', which can last for up to three weeks and leave long-lasting stains around your house.

- Eradicates the risk of testicular and uterine cancers and infections.

- Removes any risk of unwanted pregnancies in females.

- Neutered dogs are less likely to be stolen for breeding.

Grooming

Puppies and dogs who live in domestic situations usually need regular grooming, which varies depending on their breed. Mud, sand, dirty water and all the other things they pick up in their coats and between their paws on their walks can cause them irritation or harm, and are not generally the kinds of things most of us want around the house. Nor is all the hair that they naturally shed. Regular grooming is a great way to keep their coats clean and clot-free. It's also a great way to keep insects and other unwanted visitors out of their coats. Like cleaning their teeth, it is as much about preventing unwelcome health issues as it is about aesthetics. Groom your dog, and you may spot problems early!

It can also be a useful way to get your dog accustomed to being handled at the vets and any other situations where they might need to be picked up and handled by strangers, such as doggy day care or a dog walking service. A puppy who is unaccustomed to being handled in the right way, can see the insensitive approach of a human being's grasp as something to fear and fight against. So, put simply, regular grooming can also improve the quality of your dog's life.

In recent years we've seen the world of pooch pampering explode and if you have watched my show *Dogs Behaving Very Badly* on television, you'll know I've met plenty of dogs (and their owners) for whom hair styling, dressing up and even driving their own doggy car is (apparently!) an important part of their lives. I don't have anything against this kind of thing, as long as it never involves pain or discomfort for the dog and makes everyone involved happy. And as long as it is not at the cost of the kind of fundamental grooming that contributes to your dog's good health. There is little point in your puppy having pink hair one day if it is all going to fall out the next because they can't tolerate the dye.

So, think carefully before embarking on any kind of overly complicated beauty regime. And for your dog!

A WORD ABOUT DOCKING

Tail docking is considered to be a mutilation and has been illegal under UK law since 2007. There are some exemptions, such as removal of the tail by a vet for medical reasons or for certain breeds of working dogs, whose tails can be a hazard to them in their work. If you are looking at puppies whose tails have been docked for aesthetic reasons, this will have been done illegally and you should consider whether this is the right breeder to be buying a puppy from.

What is grooming, then?

At a basic level, it's simply brushing your dog's coat. But it can also mean washing them in the bath and drying them with a towel. Some dogs with long hair will need to be clipped and even have their hair blow-dried. Others who wear neckerchiefs or ribbons in their hair will need to be able to stand patiently while these accessories are added to the final look.

You'll be able to discuss your dog's individual needs with your vet. Facebook pages for your dog's breed are also a great resource when it comes to sharing tips and advice on grooming specific coats and sizes. But there are some fundamental things to consider and do when grooming. With these in place, you should find yourself with a puppy who is happy to be handled and enjoys the grooming process almost as much as you do:

- Introduce brushing your puppy's fur from as soon as they come home. It doesn't need to be thorough or involve putting any pressure on them or their body at all. It is simply to get them used to the idea that they get tickled with this brush occasionally and that it is quite enjoyable.

- Do it after a busy period of exercise; after a walk or playing in the garden is the perfect time. This way they will be tired and more likely to accept being brushed. It also sets up the idea for later life when you bring them home covered in mud and need to clean them up.

- Praise them while you are brushing them, which lets them know it makes you happy when they let you do this.

- Slow, calm hands will feel reassuring and keep your puppy steady.

- Short sessions, rewarded with a treat or a quick game with a toy, will help create positive associations.

- Build up the amount of time you spend brushing them. No puppy will sit happily for an hour while you do this. Be realistic about what they can tolerate.

- Mix up the situations in which you groom your puppy. Try putting them on a table or in front of the living room fireplace.

- Keep it easy and positive. Hurt them by snagging a knot the first time you groom them, and they'll remember for the rest of their lives!

- If they seem unhappy or try to bite the brush, simply tell them *NO* and leave it for now. Come back again and try with a shorter period of brushing or after a particularly long burst of energy, when they are feeling more relaxed.

- Avoid brushing their head and ears. Dog's heads are full of all their most vital senses and organs, which makes them extremely sensitive.

To wash or not to wash?

Just as there is with human hair, there is a school of thought that says we do not need to wash our puppy's hair with chemical shampoos and products. Dogs lived happily for millennia without getting their hair washed and come with all the necessary follicles, oils and mechanisms built in for maintaining a strong and healthy coat. It rains, after all.

However, as a race, we humans have never been more hygienic and so the hygiene of our pets has also become key. This is especially true for those of us who live in small spaces with our dogs. And even if you don't wash your dog regularly, there will be times when it is wholly necessary to rinse off whatever it is they have been rolling in!

Whether you choose to do it as a regular thing or on an as-and-when basis, here are some tips for making the process go as smoothly (and drily) as possible:

- Use lukewarm water. Too hot or too cold will be very uncomfortable for them.

- Use a natural shampoo that is designed specifically for puppies and their skin. This is not the time to be substituting the shampoo with the washing-up liquid.

- Lots of praise will let them know you are happy with them for remaining calm.

- Don't keep them in the water any longer than is necessary.

- If you have a small dog, a kitchen sink gives you more control and room than a bath.

- Have a big towel ready and give them a really good rub as soon as they get out. They will almost certainly do their own big shake as they would when they get out of a river or the sea, so avoid the splatter of dirty dog bath water in your home with a big towel dry before they shake.

- If you're not sure how often to wash them, go for once a month at first. You can add in more frequent baths if you have an exceptionally muddy puppy or fewer if it seems like they don't need it.

PERFECTLY IMPERFECT PUPPY

Some Common Puppy Ailments

Fleas, ticks and worms

This little gang of nasties are the most common parasites your puppy can attract and if not managed properly, they can cause itching, sore skin and allergic reactions. Ticks come with the added threat of being able to transmit diseases, so you really want to avoid them. Prevention is better than cure when it comes to parasites. Your vet will offer a range of preventative treatments and you can also pick up products at your local pet shop.

Diarrhoea

Young dogs are prone to upset tummies. Often, it's because they've eaten something they shouldn't, like a plant or something they've scavenged out of the compost bin. Stress, perhaps if you are moving home or have been away, can also affect their bowels. If it starts to happen frequently or you notice anything unusual, such as blood, contact your vet. Gastric problems caused by a blockage can be dangerous.

Kennel cough

Kennel cough is so-called because it's extremely contagious and spreads very quickly in group situations, such as kennels and day care. This is a respiratory disease characterised by a distinctive dry, retching cough. Other symptoms include a runny nose and gammy eyes. If your puppy is very young and has a weaker immune system, kennel cough can be especially dangerous. Ask your vet about vaccinating against kennel cough.

Parvovirus

Parvovirus is not a nice thing at all. It's a highly contagious virus that causes severe gastroenteritis and can sometimes lead to fatal complications. Symptoms include diarrhoea, vomiting, lethargy and weight loss. If you have any inkling that your puppy might have parvovirus, you need to contact your vet immediately. Because it's so contagious, you also need to be extra careful around their poo as it can be spread by humans and other animals.

Mange

Mange is a highly contagious skin disease that's caused by mites burrowing under the skin and laying eggs – ew! It causes extremely itchy skin and is highly contagious. Adult dogs usually catch mange through contact with other dogs. Mothers can also pass it on to puppies, whose weaker immune systems aren't able to fight it as well. Look out for rashes, hair loss and crusty skin. Your vet can prescribe treatment for mange, which will help it clear up, usually in a month or so.

I'm always conscious that puppies can't talk to us and tell us how they are feeling, particularly if they are ill. So if you have any doubts whatsoever about your puppy's health or wellbeing, contact a vet.

Like you and everyone else who lives in your home, your puppy will benefit from some basic hygiene and grooming rituals. Check you're delivering on these key points and your puppy will look and feel fantastic!

Key Points

- Prevention is always better than cure.

- Brushing their teeth is vital for good oral health and fresh puppy breath.

- Start brushing their coat as early as possible.

- Grooming is a great way to normalise being handled and to spot any lumps and bumps.

- Accessories are fine but safety and comfort is always most important!

Next Step

Practise, practise, practise – keep on implementing the techniques that you've already learned over the last few chapters and watch your young 'un grow from a wee pup to a much larger (or only slightly bigger, depending on the breed) four-legged friend.

NOTES

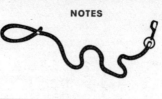

Chapter 7

Dog Days (or when they start to grow up)

*Saying goodbye to your puppy and
hello to your grown-up dog*

When is a puppy no longer a puppy?

(No, this is not one of my jokes!) Officially, the answer is when they are one year old. Vets and dog food manufacturers and pretty much every product or service you can buy for your dog, tend to see the 12-month mark as the official transition from puppy to worldly-wise adult dog.

The proper answer, of course, is that putting a time on it is kind of arbitrary. Dogs are all different and have staggeringly varied life expectancies. Great Danes, for example, live for around eight years. While some terriers can reach the grand old age of twenty! These two dogs can be born on the same day and eight years later, one can be at the end of its life and the other not yet even middle-aged.

There's also a thing called temperament. Many puppies continue to behave in a puppy-like way well into their third and fourth year. While some dogs seem to become pensioners overnight. The old nature-versus-nurture question is never far from view with dogs, and much of your puppy's behaviour and general demeanour is influenced not only by genetics but also by how they are treated and interacted with at home.

Anecdotally, I've observed that when there are children and lots of opportunities for play in the home, dogs can seem to stay young in spirit longer, compared to a dog who is a companion for an elderly person who lives alone, for example. It varies from breed to breed, dog to dog, and lifestyle to lifestyle.

One thing we can say with certainty, however, is that dogs do experience a period of adolescence. And as with any human adolescents you may have encountered, they can become surprisingly challenging!

Adolescence happens at different ages for different dogs. It can be as early as five months in some dogs and around seven or eight months in others.

In male dogs, you'll notice that they begin to cock their leg to mark their territory as testosterone levels rise, and they might become pushy, or even aggressive, with other male dogs they encounter. Female dogs will come into their first season (if they are not spayed), and you may notice some genuine changes in their mood and willingness to cooperate.

Both sexes will become more independent, and less inclined to please you, their owner. This can mean not responding to you when you ask them to do something, exploring further and wider afield on walks and not coming back when called, or perhaps being confrontational with other dogs as they grow in both their confidence and physicality. It can all be a bit of a shock if you're not expecting it, and quite disheartening when you have spent such a long time working with them on good behaviour!

The expectations of other dog owners can also be difficult to manage. We all want our dogs to behave impeccably when we are in the park or on a walk. When your adolescent pup refuses to come back to you and you feel worried that they are being burdensome playing with someone else's dog, or maybe they've stolen someone else's ball and don't want to give it back, it can all begin to feel incredibly embarrassing and awkward. Most dog owners are sympathetic and will likely have been in your shoes at some point themselves. But there are always one or two who will judge you and make you feel like the worst dog owner in the world.

My message to you here is: do not lose heart. Your puppy has not forgotten all that hard work, or been possessed by the spirit of a demon, even if at times it feels that way. This is a normal part of their development and it's important that you don't lose your temper or punish them for it. If other owners complain that your dog is not under control, simply explain that you are in the process of training and your dog is going through their adolescence. If you feel yourself becoming frustrated or unable to manage the situation, it's perfectly OK to put your puppy on the lead and call it a day for now. It is never worth letting things escalate and potentially creating a negative situation. Puppy training is challenging, and no one, especially your puppy, is perfect. Don't forget that there are many reputable professional dog trainers who can help, too.

The good news is that dogs do come out of the other side of adolescence, and all of the hard work you have put in during the early stages of their life will really begin to pay off.

🎾 *TIP:* Adolescence is a good time to introduce a longer lead. Long training leads allow your puppy to explore and be further away from you without fear of losing them. When playtime is over and it is time to walk on the pavement again, you can revert to a short lead held in a J shape, as we learned about in lead-walking on page 123.

My other message here is that puppy training never really ends. I mean this in a good way, of course! As your dog grows and becomes the well-mannered and lovely companion you have so diligently raised, you'll find that new experiences and situations crop up almost every day. Whether it's a new postman at the door, a house move or even a new younger brother or sister – human or canine – new opportunities for socialisation and revisiting many of the principles outlined in this book present themselves to you and your dog all the time. My motto here: use it or lose it! Seize every opportunity to bed-in and reinforce all the good behaviour your puppy has learned.

In particular, you should continue to make sure your dog gets to mix regularly with other dogs, and also gets to socialise in a wide variety of situations. If you

PERFECTLY IMPERFECT PUPPY

can continue to go to regular training classes, this is ideal, but if that's not possible, simply giving your dog a broad experience of daily life will help to maintain that lovely, confident demeanour you have worked so hard to cultivate. Take them with you to the pub (good excuse!), to meet friends for lunch, and even to work if you can. We have never lived in such dog-friendly times; it can only be a good thing for all of us.

Group walks are a great way to ensure your dog stays sociable while also exercising them. There are many walking groups for specific breed owners (check social media or your local pet shop), or you can set one up with other local dog owners and friends. It often means they get double the walk, with all the extra chasing and rolling around they do with their puppy pals. It can also get them used to the idea of walking and being walked by other people, which will come in handy for when you need to be away or at work. Remember to always carry poo-bags and behave responsibly when it comes to picking up after your dog.

You should also maintain regular visits to the vet and keep up to date with all their vaccination boosters, teeth brushing and general maintenance. I've said prevention is better than cure a few times in this book and I'll say it once again for good measure: prevention *really* is better than cure. Regularly spending a few minutes paying attention to your dog's wellbeing can help you avoid a lot of misery at the vets further down the line.

As you and your pup grow older and wiser together, you'll learn to tackle new challenges together, speaking the language that flows between you so easily. There are no guarantees that things will always go to plan, but with everything you have learned on the way, you can rest assured that your puppy will repay all of your time and input by being a devoted and loving friend who never fails to raise a smile. And while they may never be quite perfect, they will always be perfectly imperfect to you.

That's it, you're all set! If you get stuck or need any help, refer back to the checklists and remember that consistency, patience and kindness are all key when helping your pup make the transition to an adult dog.

Key Points

- All dogs mature at different times.

- Training is a lifelong process.

- Adolescence can be challenging, but it's a phase.

- Health checks and a healthy lifestyle are key.

- You've got a best friend for life.

Next Step

The world of dogs, and especially puppies, has its own vocabulary that can sometimes be confusing! In the next section I've put together a glossary of some of the terms you will come across when you're looking for and rearing a puppy.

Graeme's Puppy Glossary

The world of dogs has its own language, which like all language is ever growing and changing. As a student I studied languages, and so as a linguist I have always enjoyed the vocabulary and terminology that surrounds the canine community. Did you know there's now even an internet language known as DoggoLingo? This includes a whole new dictionary of words supposedly used by dogs when they're talking in memes and online videos.

I won't go into DoggoLingo here, but I thought it would be useful to include some of the many words and phrases you'll come across when looking for and rearing a puppy. This is only a very small selection of the literal thousands of words and phrases professionals use every day in their work with dogs. I've tried to stick to the ones I think will be important to you when considering your puppy choices: words for coat colours, tails, techniques and a few that are just plain silly. My favourite? Pantaloons! For more puppy vocabulary, the Kennel Club is a good place to start.

Apricot
Light, peachy coat colour, often seen in poodles and cockerpoos.

Bitch
A female dog.

Breed standard
The characteristics of an ideal breed specimen as outlined and approved by the Kennel Club.

Cross-breed
A dog who is the result of two of more different breeds.

Dam
The female parent of a litter of puppies (aka the mum).

Entire
An unneutered, male dog with two testicles.

Fawn
A light brown coat colour that often has a 'brilliance' or a subtle shine to it.

Furnishings
The long hair that some dogs get on their heads, tails and legs. Also sometimes referred to as 'feathers'.

Generalisation

Teaching your dog the same behaviour in different settings, like sitting in your kitchen and sitting at the side of the road.

Grizzle

A blue-ish or dark steely grey coat colour.

Litter

The group of puppies given birth to by a dam.

Liver

A dark shade of brown coat colour that is usually accompanied by a brown nose. Spaniels spring to mind (no pun intended!).

Mask

The dark shading on a dog's face, often seen in boxers, pugs and bulldogs.

Merle

Also known as 'dapple'. Splash-like spotting against a lighter coat background. Often seen in collies.

Mongrel

In common parlance, a dog with no definable type or breed (aka a 'mutt').

Pads

Little pads of tissue covered with thick, usually dark skin on the underside of the paws.

Pantaloons
The long, thick hair seen on the rear of some dogs' back thighs (aka 'trousers').

Ring tail
A long tail that ends in a circle.

Roan
A darker coat colour (red, brown or black) interspersed all over with another, lighter, colour. A term also found in knitting, according to my mum.

Runt
A term often used to describe the smallest and/or weakest puppy in a litter.

Sable
A coat colour describing hair that has black tips, like a fur coat.

Screw tail
A short, twisted tail that looks like a corkscrew.

Sire
The male parent of a litter of puppies.

Smooth coat
A coat with short, close-lying hair that is smooth to the touch.

Spay
The process of neutering a female dog.

Temperament
The natural qualities and traits that make up a dog's innate character.

Variable Reward Schedule (VRS)
Rewarding your dog in a random way – either a random number of times, or after a random period of time – to reinforce the idea that they will sometimes be rewarded for the desired behaviour and other times not. This builds faith in the long-term goal, which is for the behaviour to happen without any reward at all. Also known as the 'jackpot effect'.

Wheaten
A pale fawn coat colour (like wheat, funnily enough).

Whelping
The word for when a pregnant female dog (a bitch) gives birth to her puppies. She will often give birth in a whelping box and spend the first few days and weeks of her puppies' life in there as it feels safe and protected.

Wire coat
Thick, brush-like coat that feels like wire wool.

Acknowledgements

Where do you start? This book took a lot more than Yorkshire Tea, custard creams and a laptop to produce. It's been, as an old boss of mine was fond of saying, 'a team game' (copyright David Brady c 1995!). In particular, I'd like to thank everyone at Penguin and my agents, M&C Saatchi Merlin, for their help at every stage. It's no exaggeration to say I couldn't have done it without your support.

Finally, thank you, dear reader, for choosing my book. Chances are you've got yourself a new puppy or are doing your research before taking the plunge. Well, good for you! There's little in life as rewarding as bringing up a happy and healthy dog. So, here's to you, your perfectly imperfect puppy, and all of the adventures that lie ahead. Have fun!

Graeme
Cotswolds, December 2021

The publisher would like to thank Sarah Thompson for her research and work on the book.

Index

INDEX

i

illnesses 64, 155, 168–70
impulse buying 16–17
'in season' 161, 175
Irish setter 7, 161
Irish wolfhound 8

j

J-shape hold (lead-
walking) 129, 130, 134
Jack Russell 8, 22, 45–6,
60–1
joint care 40

k

Kennel Club 24, 184
and buying pedigree
puppies 21–2
and dog breed
categories 8–9
Kennel Club-
registered breeders
21–2, 26
and puppy classes 94
kennel cough 155, 168

l

labradoodle 22
Labradoodle Association

24
Labrador 12, 35, 65–6
language use 35–6
lead-walking 123–35, 177
and bad behaviour
65–6
first walks 132–4
giving proper focus to
133
and the ideal dog
position 131, 134
and the J-shape hold
129, 130, 134
and right-/left-hand-
side positioning 127
and slowing down 132
and speeding up 132
and turning left 131
and turning right
131–2
leads 48–9
leptospirosis 155
levator anguli oculi
medialis 6
licences, breeder 20
life expectancy 12, 174
litter 186
liver coat 186
lockdown dogs 27–8
looks **11**, 15
prioritization by

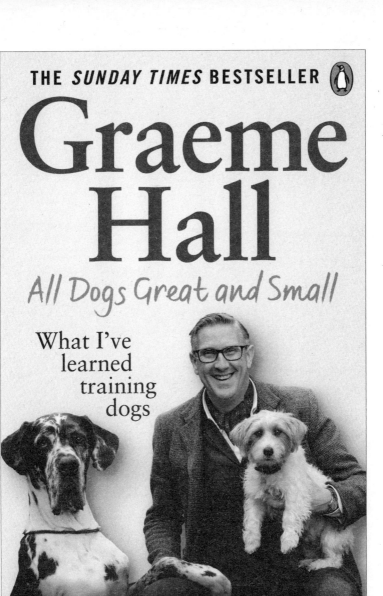